Writers of the Portuguese Diaspora in the United States and Canada:
An Anthology

Edited by
Luis Gonçalves & Carlo Matos

To

João Reboque and Angelina Pavão

and

Julie and Lucinda Gonçalves

TABLE OF CONTENTS

PREFACE

A WORD ON DIASPORAS
AND THE ANTHOLOGY

Diaspora, as I understand it, refers to the dispersal of beings in large enough hordes to specific places. In this sense, there have been, historically, many diasporas, and it is my fond hope that there will never cease to be diasporas, for ultimately, despite the exigencies and necessities that propel them, they are evidence of the persistence of hope in the human being. Anthologies, as the whole world knows, are simply collections of works selected and arranged according to an identifiable, more or less common, principle.

Having said this, I now turn to *Writers of the Portuguese Diaspora in the United States and Canada: An Anthology*, selected and arranged by the teacher–writers Luis Gonçalves and Carlo Matos. Their call to potential contributors allowed for self–identification with the diasporic group of those Portuguese who had emigrated to the northern hemisphere of this so–called New World, and their descendants. As I recall, the editors made few or no restrictions, none as to the number of texts that could be submitted, the dates of those texts, their publication histories, or their genres. Such overall openness has enabled its editors to compile a volume notable for its generous makeup, and its generic and stylistic diversity. There is a wealth, not only of literary styles, but of a whole range of interests and intentions. Thus this anthology makes for itself a complementary place in what is, as I see it, a broader effort to find a place in the sun for what until recently was an exercise, usually by one individual or two, working pretty much alone, to argue that something like Portuguese–American literature actually existed. The early efforts of Nancy T. Baden, Onésimo T. Almeida, Vamberto

Freitas and one or two others, to call attention to the existence of a literature produced by the Portuguese in the New World has resulted finally, in recent years, in gatherings of evidentiary examples into several published works, such as *Luso–American Literature: Writing by Portuguese–Speaking Authors in North America* (2011), *The Gávea–Brown Book of Portuguese–American Poetry* (2012), and *Memória: An Anthology of Portuguese Canadian Writers* (2013). And now, herewith, is *Writers of the Portuguese Diaspora in the United States and Canada: An Anthology.* That there is a place in the literary traditions of the New World for the writings of the Portuguese–speaking emigrants, the Portuguese–Americans, and their U.S. and Canadian descendants is the most important message that the existence of these anthologies sends out.

It is inevitable, I suppose, that every critic, every reviewer, and (most, perhaps) serious readers of an anthology would make some changes—additions, omissions, substitutions—in the anthology under scrutiny. After all, whether they are conscious of it or not, readers create "anthologies" of the mind by the choices of what they read and choose to reread. By recognizing such writers and offering samples of their writing, however, published anthologies help to establish and define specifically ethnic literary genres within the realm of an over–arching national or literary genre and in large compass the institution of literature itself.

In answering the editors' call for contributions to this anthology, the writers who responded by offering some of their work self–identified themselves as Portuguese–American or Portuguese–Canadian. Some of them offered poems and stories that worked with what may be called "Portuguese in North America" themes, motifs, memes, tropes, words. Others offered work that is less or even not at all "Portuguese" specific. After all, the largest cover for what is included in this work is the rubric "Writing," given that it includes, not only poetry and fiction, but history, personal testament, essay–meditation, and apologia. Not all of the pieces, strictly speaking, would generally be classified as literature. But as the work of self–identified members of the Portuguese North American diaspora down to the second and third generations–born, casting their nets wide, they do the work, individually and collectively, of this broadly conceived anthology. Writers could choose what they considered to be their best work, or, as I suspect some did in this case, choose to offer examples of their latest work. Thus the diversity of criteria open to the authors represented here in choosing their texts for inclusion in this anthology, and the resulting diversity among the texts, something less likely when the criteria for inclusion have been less inclusively spelled out by the editors. In the wide–ranging and eclectic selection of works in this volume we see traction in our quest for the genuine literature produced in our shared space by Portuguese emigrants and their descendants. It is our task, our duty, to keep it going. More names, more titles, more anthologies.

George Monteiro

January 14, 2014

KATHERINE VAZ

Katherine Vaz is a former Briggs-Copeland Fellow in Fiction at Harvard and a Fellow of the Radcliffe Institute. Her novels include *Saudade*, selected in the Barnes & Noble Discover Great New Writers series, and *Mariana*, in six languages, selected by the Library of Congress as one of the Top 30 International Books of 1998. *Fado & Other Stories* won the 1997 Drue Heinz Prize and *Our Lady of the Artichokes* received the 2007 Prairie Schooner Prize. Her short fiction has appeared in dozens of magazines, and her children's stories have been included in anthologies from Simon & Schuster, Penguin, and Viking. Vaz received a National Endowment for the Arts Fellowship and is the first Portuguese–American to have her work recorded for the Library of Congress. She was appointed to the six–person U.S. Presidential Delegation at the World's Fair in Lisbon.

Taking a Stitch in a Dead Man's Arm

I changed the bandage over my father's knee in the final month of his life. His wound was purple, and blood heaved through. I never looked away from it. I swallowed my vomit when it struck the back of my clenched teeth; I was ready to swallow my insides as often as necessary—it was important to gaze at his flesh exactly as it was because I would not have it with me for much longer. I wanted to learn matter–of–factness about being this close to someone. The yellow fluid on the gauze around the bloodstains, the cortisone spray that would have made Papa scream if he'd had the strength: my stain, my shock and my scream.

A brain lesion gave him double vision. Everything wore a register of itself, a crown of haze. It amused him to watch people walking around with the ghosts of themselves stuck to their skins. Papa's knee had ripped open when he fell off a ladder while trying to repair a broken window sash. Frantic to protect us, to seal every entry, he had crawled from his sick bed while my mother was at work at the Sunshine Biscuit factory and I was at school. A killer who called himself the Zodiac was roaming the Bay Area. He was sending letters with obscene ciphers to *The San Francisco Chronicle*.

"Isabel," said my father, his fingers brushing first the specter of my face and then my face. The rind of the moon cut through the windowpane. The wallpaper was an old pattern of "The Strawberry Thief," with sharp birds poking through tall red grasses. Saint Anthony of love and lost things had an arm span covering the top of the bureau, and someone had sent over a plug–in picture, with a light bulb in the back, of Saint Lucy with her plate of eyeballs. Papa was forty–two; he would stay posed in time with black hair.

He did not know how to guard me anymore. He could no longer hide the newspapers, as he did when Richard Speck murdered those nurses in Chicago. *Fear gives off a smell. That's how evil finds its victims, Isabel. If you don't give it off, you'll be safe, you won't get hurt in the dark.*

I told him he must stop worrying. The Zodiac would not bother coming to our town: What was here? Every morning I walked to the Boulevard to catch the bus to Bishop Delancy High School in Oakland, and we passed the Adobe Feed Store, where my father had said that hiding in the sacks were eggs, smaller than the eye could see, waiting to hatch into vermin. And sometimes I had caught it, in the days of holding his hand when we went to buy chicken scratch. The sacks jumped, they stirred a bit, moth wings straining against the weight of the feed. Eggs and wings: I thought of death as white. Our morning bus passed the Miniature Golden–Tee, with its hydra–head of neon dragons guarding the windmills, clowns with big mouths waiting for a golf ball to gag them, and a little wild–west corral with a gate that gave out a horse whinny again and again as it swung open. What was in San Damiano? It sounds like a place with terracotta earth and a Spanish mission, but it was an ordinary suburb, house after house with those netless basketball hoops, with a gauntlet of stores on San Damiano Boulevard. People favored wind chimes in the shape of pagodas, which they bought in Chinatown in San Francisco, as if crossing the bridge was going from part A of the world to part B, and the winds blew in and tilted the pagodas and no one ever straightened them; there was always a faint music, a trickle, really, coming from these shattered columns of pagodas.

I was in love with someone who was leaving me his own lessons in being unafraid. James was a tall Filipino boy in my sophomore class who wore three–piece business suits on Free Dress Day and smoked cigars with the Asian kids in the parking lot, and once when Sonny Barger and some Hells Angels rode through, as they did now and then, James threw a flaming butt end at one of them and got flipped off but not hurt. I understood that the motorcyclist admired James for a moment, and it thrilled me, to watch how someone could go straight toward points of fear.

Violet Wong, my best friend, would get onto the bus with me at the San Damiano stop, and she'd take out the green eye shadow that she'd stolen from her mother. We'd put it on with our fingers, and my lashes were so long that they stroked green dust onto the inside of my glasses. She wanted to help me be beautiful for James.

I had written a speech for him, and he won the regional Lions Club contest with it and would go on to state finals. He had not told me that he won; one of his friends did, and when I went to him, he said, "I was going to tell you, Isabel." I wanted him to bury his face in my hair and wet my scalp with his mouth, to breathe my name back to me inside my ear.

How could I explain any of this to my father—the odd, awful timing of my love?

I'm not scared of anything, Papa. That was all I could manage. "That's good!" he whispered. "I don't want you taking a stitch in my arm."

"No, I won't, Papa," I said, and we laughed.

It was a joke between us. When he was a boy on the island of São Miguel in the Azores, he suffered with a fear of the dark. His mother had explained to him that the cure for that in her family, she was very sorry to say, was taking a stitch in a dead man's arm.

The cure was horrible, but its strength lasted forever. "Forever" had sounded wonderful to my father, so he said yes, next time there was a dead man in the town of Sete Cidades, he would take a stitch in his arm. Nothing could be worse than the monsters roving in his bedroom at night.

My father was five years old. His mother stood outside the chapel, crying into a lace handkerchief. Since fear of the dark is fear of aloneness, my father had to go by himself to the dead man in his casket. The thread in the needle was white. Papa thought the man looked like marzipan, especially where a drip of pink paint stood out on his ear.

He had died from falling off a stone wall, where he had been entwining hydrangeas through the gaps. Everyone agreed that the world fought back when you tried to make it beautiful.

My father pulled up the young dead man's cuff and touched a waxy arm. His name was Jaime, and his mustache was trimmed neatly for the first time ever. My father stuck the needle into the wrist and pushed until it dipped through flesh and emerged from under the skin, and then he thought, all right, that's enough. Two drops of fluid seeped at the prick marks. My father's stomach shrank smaller than a fist. He left the thread in the man's skin and drew his sleeve down and ran back to his mother.

It was easy to give up fear of darkness rather than repeat such a cure. Maybe it was some old–world remnant, sticking a man with a needle to make certain that he was not merely in a coma. At one funeral in Sete Cidades, a man had bolted upright in his coffin while being borne to the cemetery and roared, "How will I breathe underground?"

Maybe the idea was to stitch the body to earth, so that it would not cling with its worms to the spirit trying to fly to heaven.

Death sinks a person's eyes back until they become bright creatures in a tide pool.

I got up to go to my room, and my father grabbed my arm and said, "Don't leave me, Isabel! Not yet," and I saw, on the gleam of fever, on the water on his eyes, a terrible fear, and I did not know if it might be from him, or if it were my own, reflecting back to me. Perhaps I was so far into fright that I'd touched clear round to the other side, where I could claim to be past it;

perhaps I was a liar; I could stand that. But I could not bear to think that the fear might be coming from him.

For once I did not mind Mama's habit every night of getting out our glow–in–the–dark rosary set. The Holy Family statute had a hollow compartment to house the rosary.

I held it under a lamp's light to turn the beads into glowworms. My mother snapped off the lights, and she, my father, and I handed the fluorescent beads from one grasp to another in the dark. Fingering this string of lights like the souls of infant stars, I finally knew what to pray: *I'll give up love, if You'll save my father.*

That was my bargain with God.

*

Our Alameda County transit bus, #80, went from San Damiano through San Leandro and then under the "Free Huey" banners along East 14th Street into Oakland. Near the General Motors plant, we picked up the riders going to Castlemont High, near Bishop Delancy. They had Afros with Fro–Piks stuck in them and wore Angela–Davis glasses and hiphugger lace–up football pants, including the girls, with angel–flight hems.

On their Pee–Chee folders, they had penciled dashikis and black–haloed hair over the waspy white kids in tennis outfits. We lifted our schoolbooks onto our laps to free up seats for them.

One day Charles Mayer, a Castlemont Knight with his purple–and–white letterman's jacket, sat next to me. Everyone knew him from his picture in the newspaper.

He was heading for the NBA. He ripped out a sheet of binder paper from a folder and began writing in pencil. Out of the corner of my eye, I saw his writing, and I did not know what came over me when I leaned over and said, "No, 'receive' is 'ei,' not 'ie.'"

I cringed when he said, "What?" and looked right at me. I glanced near his eyes and told him about the spelling of 'receive.' He jotted it down and insisted it didn't look right, but I told him, Believe me, I'm sorry for speaking to you, I didn't mean it, but I'm telling you the truth: Receive.

Charles Mayer handed me his paper and said, "What else is wrong here. Tell me."

Every day after that, I moved my books for him to sit where I could help with his homework. Once when some Castlemont kids pried up a bus seat and crammed it out a window to protest the arrest of Eldridge Cleaver, and the Delancy kids were jostled around, Charles Mayer told them not to touch me. It had nothing to do with the usual sort of love; that was understood. He had a girlfriend and plenty of other girls after him. I was ugly, with my skinniness and battles against fright. We all rolled our blue herringbone tweed skirts at the waist in a gruesome attempt to have mini–skirts. He was taking a portion of my mind, but not as James had. One morning Charles handed me five pralines made by his grandmother, in a baggie secured with a psychedelic–streaked rubber band.

He said, "Thanks—tell me your name?"

"Isabel Dias," I said.

"Isabel Dias," he said, as if pleased with locating an obscure country on a map. "I got a B on my essay about my future," he said.

My hand was moist around the bag with the pralines.

"Thank you," I said.

"No problem, thank *you*," he said, and we each settled back into our books.

In that essay, he had written: *This is my world at this moment. Everyone I meet is my history. This is the year that Charles Mayer has stepped into his life.*

When we disembarked at Delancy, Violet said, "What's wrong, Isabel?" I ran to the rest room, willing to let the smokers beat me silly, and I locked myself into a stall and wept, I wept without making noise, I was good at that; imagine me counting just a tiny bit as someone's history. How uncanny, too, that my father should seep inside my lonely hours: with the raw instincts of a small animal, with the Zodiac on the loose, I found myself a protector on the bus, a guardian angel on his way to money and fame, far, far above anything I was, but I counted now in his tally of moments, owing to my lack of fear in spelling out Receive.

An essay or two later, Charles Mayer stopped taking our bus. I never saw him in person again, though I continued to see his photo in the sports news. I heard that he had a car now. Rumor had it that it was a gift from a recruiter, because his future was so much on the rise.

*

I studied my mother the way I looked at the eyes and blood of my father, to preserve her as she was right then, down to the safflower oil with its faint scent that she rubbed into her skin. Already, young, her skin was overly set, like the film on a pudding, and her light brown hair was thinning, and her glance seemed not to be owning things but making blank spaces where she looked, and I forgave her. I never thought that not seeing me meant that she did not love me. She could hardly bear to look at my father. I would make watery soup but she refused it. Right through her skin it was poking out, the dryness in her bones. When she curled up next to my father on their bed, I took off her shoes and set them upright on the carpet, where they exhaled her entire day of standing and picking the pink marshmallow cookies off the conveyor belt and putting them bottom to bottom inside the compartments of a box. The Sunshine people let the workers eat all they wanted, but one week we had devoured four boxes of pink cookies and three boxes of Sunshine cheese crackers on purpose, to break the habit of wanting any more.

Mama, dozing next to my father, would give a startled shudder of remembering me, and with her eyes still shut, not looking at either of us for fear of dying of it, she let me crawl between her and Papa. Their silver carpet was bare, stripped to its gums. Somehow the roses on the carpet had worn themselves onto the bottoms of our shoes but since we saw no roses on our shoes I think they must have gone up into our feet, roses inside my mother's feet and climbing inside her sore calves as she stood at the factory.

When I roused myself to go off to my own bed, I could not sleep. Suddenly the dark drifted into a white blindness, like the belly of a night turned inside out. I got up in the white sac of night to clean the green leather couch, Comet on a rag that made the green pale. The majolica Christ child over the stove, inside His ring of majolica fruit, had collected streaks of grease, too far to reach.

I piled bedclothes on top of myself and put my arms and legs around them and thought of them as a man, and I thrust around like a stupid fish on land, and that made me feel worse, because a man would move in ways beyond predicting. Even then I suspected that when a woman got to be experienced in love, that was the point—for him to surprise you; the very touch of love was a plunging reminder of the unknown, the same unknown I carried with me now.

*

21

I heard that James came in third in the state finals of the speech contest held by the Lions Club. I was about to round the corner to find him at his locker, to tell him that he had gone quite far with my speech and should not think of it as failing. I decided this would not violate my vow to give him up. I stopped when I heard his voice say, "Deborah, I'm dying to fuck you." And thereafter I saw him with this girl, who had long blonde hair that she plaited and undid so that it held a ripple. Her rouge compact fell out in the bathroom and I kept it: Mauve Turbulence.

In religion class, Sister Miriam showed a filmstrip about sex, in which a priest's voice–over affixed every act of physical love onto a scale. "Looking at, talking to, walking with" was at the end marked "Early Stage of Arousal." "S.I."—for "sexual intercourse"—was at the far other end, in the Marriage part of the scale. The projector went "Ping!" whenever Sister Miriam had to move the filmstrip. The narrating priest said, cheerily, "I really don't know where to put the fondling of the breasts!" and the screen showed an "f" surrounded by question marks that ended up straddling the line between Engagement and Marriage.

So God was merely amused. I had not even been on the scale with James. I had not owned this love enough for me to offer it up. And the pain I was in meant I had not even truly surrendered the nothing I had. But what of any of it? My father might be saved now, but there comes a time when such a prayer is always laughed at.

My lungs flattened so that it was impossible to get air into the bellows of them. I took an early bus home and crawled onto the bed where my father lay with his pounding double vision. I did not speak; I tried to get some breath into me so I would not die. He put his hand on my hair—kindly, though I had failed him. My glasses fell off and the birds on the wall, the strawberry thieves, blurred into a red ironworks; it was almost pretty. He said that he'd been wrong his whole life; taking a stitch in a dead man's arm hadn't been about fear of the dark.

Was I listening to him? Was I?

I moved a shoulder a bit to signal him yes.

It was about leaving behind the curse of waiting. "Waiting is the fear you have to get over, Isabel," said my father, so lightly I barely heard him. It frightened me that he could hear my heart battering its way onto the sheet. "Don't wait for anyone." Because waiting was darkness, having no imagination to see beyond the fallen curtain, where you were right then. But when you were young and looking at a dead man, and actually sticking it to him, you were saying that it wasn't your time to die, it was your time to enter your better and better future.

There were so many cracks in our house that I was sure that water ebbed in while we slept, filling every room to the ceiling. The Zodiac got in through one of the cracks, but we fought him, and his knife, instead of killing us, opened gills on our sides and we could breathe.

The Zodiac had a fear of drowning and swam away. My mirrored vanity plate of lavender soaps and vanilla cologne got swept up in a vortex of water. My father had been a champion ocean swimmer, and this, to him, was child's play. This was nothing, getting to dance underwater until morning, when the water receded and daylight began and a string of water was lying out of our mouths, connecting whatever had gone on in our heads in the night to our pillows.

My mother and I threw out the newspapers, though my father could no longer read. We had to protect him from the latest: The Zodiac had written a letter that said: *Ha! Ha! Ha! Your pigs can't catch me!! When a busload of Catholic kiddies step off in their uniforms I'll go pop! pop! and I am going to find me some niggers too.*

My #80 bus, with Delancy and Castlemont students, was a gift box, wrapped and delivered, for the Zodiac. Everyone thought this, but no one figured we should worry.

The Zodiac would stay in San Francisco. Surely death would not trouble itself to stalk us on this one obscure line from San Damiano to Oakland.

Death was too busy, death was in my father's body. I stitched my gaze to my father's when he yelled, "Isabel!" He looked straight into me, and I looked back, into the iris and nerves.

When he died, my mother insisted on a simple, closed–coffin affair, no flinging ourselves at the dead, no kisses that drew back embalming paint. But at his wake, I almost fainted from the smell of the casseroles, the Chinese noodles baked over ground beef and peas, the lasagnas oozing like a cutaway of magnified muscle, the Boston pies leaking their middles—I stopped eating for days, and then, all at once, my bones shook as if my father were shaking me, I saw black puddles moving along the floor and sticking together to make odd black–water animals, and I could not wait to eat, I ate, my mother said, like someone who was going to be shot in the morning.

As a girl, I had attended a school run by Carmelite nuns from Spain who told us stories about their parents being killed in the Civil War. Once a year, we filed into the convent's chapel and the priest held out a black speck housed under a glass swollen like a belly. We had to kiss the glass over this black jot, which was a particle of bone from the founder of the order.

How had this bone chip been obtained? What part of the body was it from?

Why did we turn the color of night down to our bones when we died?

There is always some way in which we lend ourselves to taking a stitch in the body of the dead. Someone had taken not a needle but a knife and carved into bones; I, for my part, had long ago stitched my breath to the glass over a fragment of a woman.

At school, Violet held out her biology book and said, "Isabel! Did you know that the skeletons in the wings of birds are the same shape as the inside of the human hand?"

That would be just like my father, to hide where he would not frighten the living.

He and the other dead could sweep across the daytime sky, over my head, caressing the face of the air.

My mother would sit in dark rooms and not move. In the living room, the dotted Swiss curtains bulged out when air blew in through the screens. It was as if the air had shape, and the curtains were stretching themselves over it. "Shall we go for a walk, Mama?" I asked, and out we ventured under the birds in the sky, stunned and silent, but at a distance I imagine we must have seemed to be striding quite fearlessly down the road. I could not rescue my father, but for now I could rescue her: I had won my bargain, it seemed; I had kept my father with me.

*

While walking down Redwood Road to the bus stop on San Damiano Boulevard, I noticed a car—maybe a station wagon—going in one driveway, pulling out, going into the driveway of the next house, pulling out. Someone was following me, entering and idling for a moment in every driveway so that he could stay behind me. I walked a little faster and stepped closer to the curb. Hardly any other cars were out at that hour, still dark, before seven. I was wearing my trench coat over my uniform, with the fringe of my herringbone skirt showing, and blue knee socks and coffee–and–cream saddle shoes.

I passed the San Damiano Library, a low glass building across from Faith Lutheran Church; the car went into its parking lot. I thought that if I took care not to look at the car, it would leave me alone. I tried a fast walk, afraid to look over my shoulder until I told myself, Fear nothing, your father is with you: Don't give off the smell of fear; that's when the larger animal will catch the smaller one. I knew how to protect myself.

The Boulevard wasn't far, and men worked all hours at the Union 76 station near the bus stop. I wondered if I should get the license plate number, or look at the man behind the wheel, but I broke into a run when I saw the gas station.

The A.C. Transit driver, Owen Campbell, was getting coffee out of the vending machine. When I ran up to him, breathing hard, I said, "There's a car back there I don't like."

Mr. Campbell and two of the station attendants walked out with me and looked down the street, but the car had vanished.

"You get the number?" asked Mr. Campbell.

I shook my head. I told him what had happened, and he put his hand on my shoulder and said, "Maybe it's just one of those things."

"Maybe," I said.

"Because it's a strange world," he said.

"That's right."

He escorted me to the bus. I told Violet that someone had come after me in my Catholic uniform, and she stifled a yell and started a whisper in the bus about the Zodiac. By the time we stopped at the General Motors plant for the Castlemont students, the fear in the bus went into their skin too, and they picked up the murmur: Of course he'd find us. We're a two–for–one deluxe murderer's dream. A girl next to me opened her Bible to the Twenty–third Psalm: He *leadeth me beside the still waters/Yea, though I walk through the valley of the shadow of death, I will fear no evil.*

She took hold of my sleeve. We did not speak, but she clutched these stitches all over my arm. I hope it made her less afraid. For me it was a sweetness out of nowhere. How close to dying it still arrives, the better and better surprise. We could be minutes from gunfire, and someone finds the time to take hold of me.

When the bus stopped at Delancy, Mr. Campbell opened the door and exited first.

He turned around and walked a bit, and then I stepped off. If the car were lurking, I would be able to identify it. It was the most fearless moment of my life. When I was out in the open, and the other students poured out, Mr. Campbell said to me, "God bless you, sweetheart," a further gift in the middle of all that fear. No one had ever called sweetheart before, not even in my family.

There was no news that day, nor on any of the following days, about the Zodiac killer. He was never found, though it was guessed years later that he might have been apprehended for a different crime. Who knows? We refuse to believe in the persistence of the sinister. Perhaps he is a clerk or a dental technician or professor, his skull's interior filled with webs that no one else can see.

Violet Wong drowned in the Bay during a marine biology trip in her freshman year at the University of California at Berkeley.

As far as I know, Charles Mayer never made it to the NBA; I hope life has not disappointed him. I hope he did not die in Vietnam. I wish him a good and cheerful family.

James came into my life twenty years after I last saw him, at an awards banquet for journalists. I was getting a small prize for some pictures I had taken. I was divorced and madly, utterly, out of my skin in love with a married man. I lived in a studio on Pine Street in San Francisco, where I developed pictures in my own darkroom. James came up to me at the banquet, and we had a drink together. But he was no longer beautiful to me, because he reminded me of what I still was—someone perpetually learning not to wait forever. There are times that contain all we shall ever be; everything we learn can be traced back to that start of the shading in of all we more fully come to know. Back then in the year when I learned to step into my life, there lay the first threads: darkness, waiting, the dragon in the landscape, love running in blood and water through my grasp.

My mother still lives in our little house with the red wallpaper in San Damiano, the sort of artless place that no one wants to admit being from, the place where I thought, What was here?

With Andrew, my married man, I gave up many things, including my notion of "here." When he came to where I lived—here, there, it didn't matter at all—anywhere was everything. He knew how to kiss the length of my spine and enter me almost at the same time and hold my head from behind so that he could feel my violent heaving face, and when I was by myself, when he went home to his wife, I was quite clear about one definite new fright. I had crested something and hit up against that farthest fear of the dark: Nothing would touch me more than this that I was about to lose. Soon he and I would end this passion simply because it refused to have an end of its own. You could take a stitch in a dead man's arm in order to defeat the night, because you wanted to live.

But what if you hit up against a love that would cling to you, so that no one else would be able to touch you directly, not ever again, because that—him, it, the hours, this created thing between you—would stay adhered?

Oh, Father. One lifetime is never enough to figure everything out, not the mystery you left off solving, the mystery that began when you were very young and took a stitch in the body of death and thought: *There it is, I've finished, I will never again be afraid of the dark.* What happens when it's you that's the body lying there alone?

AMY SAYRE BAPTISTA

Amy Sayre Baptista (the artist formerly known as Amy Sayre–Roberts) is a full–on, flat–out, tilt–of–wheel bad ass. She is descended of Madeiran immigrants and the offspring of a tornado collided with a hurricane. Soon after her birth she began eating avocados whole and writing poetry. Her most recent publications are with *Alaska Quarterly Review* and *Ninth Letter*. She has removable ears and bats left–handed.

The Fisherman's Daughter Learns To Fly

Daddy says, You don't kill it less you use it all.
He says, Salt and brains are the most important ingredients.

Preserving a deer's hide must be done correctly
or skin rots on the frame like memory.

Daddy and I stretch carcass over
plywood. I hand him nails and hold the hammer.
All that remains must be scraped away. We are gods working
in reverse. Unmaking the creature
bathed last night in moonglow, a leap as silent as rain.

I am ten and want to forget the inside smell of deer.

Stop crying or go back to the house.

I want to tip the pan of brains back into the empty skull, unskin the legs
as delicate as kindling wood, refire the heart.

You hear me?

I nod yes.

A crow swoops, grabs a string of gut and my soul reaches out for escape
Daddy puts a knife in my hand and pushes down hard on the hide
I scrape away the gore and he pulls the wind from my mouth saying
nothing
but teaching me salt is meant to swallow.

Return of the Fisherman's Daughter

I left the River for the Sea,
mapped a line from my belly to the tide—
the umbilical cord was blue.
The Sea asked, "River?"
I answered:

> *Make me over beautiful, unstitch my sides and set the cottonmouth free*
> *fill me full with seahorse and salt water.*
> *I've come down from the mountain, crossed the bluff, watched daddy sew the last seed*
> *in the universe just to give the world away.*

> *I've come down from the mountain to the Sea, watched the bluff fade flat to horizon,*
> *made the sign of the cross while daddy dipped, cried on the wind like a seabird*

> *Floods are my birthright; rising water is my sister's best friend*
> *brackish and braided, the slim–hipped girls who taught me what boys want,*
> *the way to fix my hair.*
> *So flood me, watch me rise,*
> *I woke this morning with a seahorse tattoo inside my thigh*

The Sea asked, "River?"
I answered:

> *Touch me.*
> *Touch me again, touch me*
> *at the spot behind my knee and the mountain,*
> *at the bend in the bluegrass,*
> *on the break of the wave.*
> *The first place my skin knew yours*
> *that first inch of skin*
> *where your tongue tipped the scale*
> *and woke me.*

> *I've come down from the mountain, crossed the bluff, left the shore.*
> *I waded past the panther to swim amongst the rising dead.*
> *I found daddy there, arms tangled between a tree root, a tractor tire*
> *his tongue pouring out his mouth like a serpent*
> *I cut it out, swallowed him whole.*
> *Black as bitterroot, I danced until my feet bled*
> *sweating out my superstitions,*
> *coiled, rotten as sulfur water.*

The Sea whispered, "River?"

Abandon all you know about sleep.
Skin the snake, smother the widow's return.
Threaten the sunset with knives and cymbals

Keep me awake

Until the surf pounds my body to sand.
Until the River says, home.
Until the River calls me child.

The Fisherman's Daughter Meets a Weird Sister

Chanting over the carcass of a fox, in a cave at Hog Island,
we find a river–witch. Her hair, a tangle

of fishhooks, spiderwire. You shame my scream
with fingers that stink of bait and brackish water.

You say she comes from the wildling clan and bit off
the nose of a man who tried to kiss her.

The witch sings, *God drowns the river in children and angels.*

She knives the rusted belly, reaches her hand in and brings out
two knots of fur. You say no one should interfere with nature.

She blows breath into the pups, *rip tear* and *tree root.*
The small coppers cry to life then she slices

each nipple and suckles the greedy mouths.
You cover my eyes with blushing palms.

But her tongue echoes in me like songs from a well.
Feed what hungers lest you starve.

Rock, breath, moonrise, wonder.

The Fisherman's Daughter Gets A Lesson in Meteorology

When the drought follows Spring, puffs of grey breath exhale our every
  step.
Gnats feed on farmer's blood and men open their mouths to the sky,
begging the river–witch for rain.

Hang rattlers from the Willow limbs, hook cottonmouth with Hawthornes.
Clouds follow the shadow you meet on the road to Orleans.

The men lay down bags of sugar, cords of firewood, and snapping turtle
  eggs
to pay the prophesy. When the floods come, carp feed from the
  cornfields,
men throw bladders of blood against the cave walls, and whore the witch's
  daughters.

River–witch back–tracks the tide until men piss coal water and beg for
  mercy.
She silences lamentations with laughter sharp as a skinning knife and fills
    the moon with stinkbate. The next rain is a plague, the long suck
    on a dry breast aching men's teeth.

Snakes do not sing, nor worms guard the door. Horse madness holds no remedy for
    hysteria.

When the river broke the levy, men nail her hands to a tree stump,
tie her feet to a skittish mare, bellow for thunder.

Inês De Castro Ascends the Throne

Unbury me. Reverse the dirt. Sink your arms elbow deep into the soil
    covering my body, this depth shows respect for the dead.

Pry open the coffin lid with your bare hands. Lose fingernails in the
    process. You'll need to bleed a bit to gain my forgiveness.

Pass my severed head through a Laurel's split trunk to quench the king's
    desire for revenge. Understand, that remedy is not foolproof. The
    risks you take are your own.

Lift me gently. Slowly, slowly, as not to tear the tender ghost from flesh.

Don't you dare shudder. If any piece of me falls, and you slip, and whisper
    my name, expect to suffer a thousand deaths in retribution. Now
    burn the rags hanging from my body. The smoke startles demons
    from their mischief.

At last, set me up on the throne and call the murderers forth, let every
    living thing fall from my mouth. Rename the wretched jaw beauty,
    and predict my splintered tooth a relic to divert storms at sea.

When the murderers lean down and press their lips to my feet. Split open
    their stupidity and tear it out by the roots. Let their ignorance twist
    and suffer in the dust of my bones. Let it die there.

Here's a secret between you and me: Pedro made promises he could not
    keep. Someone has to suffer for it.

Now lay down in my grave. Shroud yourself in the soil lately unearthed.
    Pray the saints will come and find you. Know, they will not reach
    you in time.

GEORGE MONTEIRO

George Monteiro is a career–long student and teacher of nineteenth– and twentieth–century American literature, contributing to the scholarship on many writers, including Edgar Allan Poe, Henry Adams, Henry James, Emily Dickinson, Edith Wharton, Stephen Crane, Ernest Hemingway, F. Scott Fitzgerald, William Faulkner, Robert Frost, T. S. Eliot and Bob Dylan. He has also translated the poetry of Fernando Pessoa, Jorge de Sena, Miguel Torga, and Pedro da Silveira. His latest books are *Elizabeth Bishop in Brazil and After: A Poetic Career Transformed* (McFarland, 2012), *As Paixões de Pessoa* (Ática, 2013), *The Gávea-Brown Book of Portuguese-American Poetry*, co-edited with Alice R. Clemente (Gávea-Brown, 2013), and *Robert Frost's Poetry of Rural Life* (McFarland, 2015).

How I Emigrated to America, the Land of My Birth

When I was eight months old I was sent into exile. Let me explain. It all begins, naturally, with family. We always had my Mother's birthday cake on the twenty–ninth of November, which should not have been a problem, except that she kept insisting, every year, that her real day of birth was the eleventh or twelfth. It always puzzled me, this not knowing your birth date for sure. Every year on the twenty–ninth, there would be cards, the small cake and the candles, and always her gracious "yes, thank you, thank you. It's a nice cake. But you know, I think my birthday is really in early November, on the eleventh, the twelfth maybe."

I could never figure that one out. Why didn't she know for sure? And of course she wouldn't think of celebrating her birthday on the eleventh or twelfth even if we tried to do it. Then one day I got an answer. It all started when she told me the story of the woman in Taunton we had just visited on Saturday. The woman had been injured in a car accident and was still recovering from her injuries.

"That woman was amazing. She worked miracles. It wasn't her fault they found out about me and Lucinda." She talked while she sewed, as she always did, not wanting, I suppose, to waste the time doing only one thing. "That was the doing of some of the old–timers who wanted to get in good with the authorities. You know who they are, the Pireses and the Cardanhas. But it's best to forget them, at least forget about what they did to us. Still, that woman—it's sad to see her now. She doesn't look powerful. Life's been tough on her, at least lately. But maybe after she gets healthy again, gets a bit stronger, she'll be all right. But she will never be her old self again."

In my mind's eye I saw this woman again, saw her as she was now— fiftyish, wrapped in a faded gray–green flannel bathrobe, her pepper–and– salt hair cut short like a man's, wearing a plain square watch with a large face set in a heavy black leather strap, the face showing out from the inside of her wrist. "Look, look at these," she bossed, holding out some newspaper clippings. "Notice the picture of the accident. Good thing that photographer came along. See how that guy's car is rammed up against the side of my car, the car I was riding in, I mean. Somebody's got to pay for all this, my injuries, my disability, my loss of working time. I've got a good lawyer. I couldn't use Andrade, of course. He's family—well as good as family—and it might hurt the case. Besides, I've got an excellent lawyer. I'll win this one. You'll see. Everybody will see. I'll win it. I'll do it."

She put the clippings down, on top of the desk, stood up straight, thumped her fist into her open hand, twice, three times, and then again leaned down to the desk, picked up the clippings, glanced at them, put them back, in a drawer this time, and pushed the drawer flush. "If I could get those boys out of the trenches, and I did get them out, I certainly did, I can win this case."

"That woman was remarkable, what she did nobody could do," said my mother, without missing a stitch, then drawing in her breath and talking to the end of her story. "That's why you were with me back in Portugal on your first birthday, that's why you took your very first steps in Freixo–de–Espada–à–Cinta where your father is from. That's why the first word you ever said, you said in Vila Ruiva da Serra. Remember that picture I keep with the other pictures in the drawer? You're walking along in the Lameiro and you're hanging on tightly to a bottle? A small brown bottle full of milk? Remember?

"What she did in the War was miraculous. One miracle after another. She pulled boys right out of the trenches in France, right out of the fighting. She got them away from the bullets, from the shells, away from the gas. How did she do it? She proved that those boys had been born in America. They were Americans who didn't belong in any foreign army. That's the way it started. But after a while things changed, and the truth was that some of the later ones that she got out of France weren't American–born at all. Some of them were children born to immigrants who had been in America all right, but they were born only after the parents had returned to Portugal.

"No, these boys were Portuguese all the way, and before they were sent to the War they hadn't even been away from their villages, let alone out of the country. How did she do it? It so happened that these boys had names similar or identical to names of other boys their age who had been born to Portuguese parents in the United States, taken back to the old country, and had the misfortune, poor things, to die in childhood. Working from the United States, that woman dug up all the papers, birth certificates and what have you, belonging to the now–dead children so that they could be used for the grown–up boys now in France. It was not an honest thing to do, of course, but it worked. And nobody was hurt by what she did.

"Now let me tell you why we—you and I—were in Portugal, marking time just six months after you were born, born right here in America, in this very house." She paused, having come to the end of that particular bit of mending, on a boy's white shirt, and bit off the thread. She folded the shirt and put it aside, and then picked up one of her own blouses, looked it over carefully, sighed, and began to sew up a tear at the sleeve, just above the cuff.

"When the War was over," she resumed her story, "that woman went back to doing whatever it was she did in peacetime. But a few years later, when they stopping allowing immigrants to come into America, she had another good idea. She decided that she knew a way to bring over young men and women. She would arrange it so that they could present themselves at the American Consulate in Lisbon as Americans and thereby escape the immigration laws. These men and women would be taught to assume new names, the names written on the American passports she finagled for them. And in that way she got them to the United States. A few of them kept right on with the new names, but for the most part these new Americans were too well-known to those immigrants who had come before them to stick to the names on their passports. Besides, some of them went by nicknames anyway. So they never used their assumed names. That was the way it was with me and Lucinda.

"She was able to do all this, and she did it for a long time, maybe three or four years. My father—your grandfather—was living in the United States by himself just about the time she was sneaking people into the country. He heard about it. People weren't supposed to talk about it, but it was an open secret. He never forgot it, and when, later, he was back in Vila Ruiva da Serra, this time for good, and he took a hard look at what his daughters were facing by way of a future, he remembered this woman who worked miracles for others. Why not for him, too, or at least for his daughters. It was not yet time to think about the youngest one, but he had two nearly grown daughters and their prospects, as far as he could tell, were so bad he had to do something for them. Naturally his thoughts ran to the woman in America who could arrange it so that they wouldn't have to spend the rest of their lives in that God forsaken village. Things those days were awful, really bad, and they were not much better in the rest of the country. Thank God his son was already in America. Maybe he could get that woman to agree to work on his daughters' behalf. Maybe. 'Please take them out of this miserable place,' he begged the woman. He had sought her out immediately when he heard that she was visiting relatives in Melo. 'I want them to go to America. When they get there they can live with their brother. You know him. He's your friend Grace's brother-in-law. We're practically family, you see. Aren't we? You'd be doing something for the family, and you'd be doing it—charity—for these girls, for me and my wife—in the sacred memory of your father and mother.' Fortunately, he told her, he could also scrape up the money to get his daughters to Lisbon, right to the ship. The passage-money itself, he assured her, would come on a loan from his son,

40

your uncle—Tio Temudo.

"In time we received 'our' passports. They were issued in names different from ours, of course, and they showed birth dates that were not ours either. It all went well. In less than a year, Lucinda and I were here, in America, living with your uncle and working in the Tamarack mills. The Tamarack closed down a long time ago, but when we started working there it was full of people like us, people of all nationalities. Hundreds, maybe thousands. That's where I met your father. He was a strong man, handsome, serious, healthy. He was older than I was, more mature. He had lost his wife many years earlier. She was only nineteen when she died, and she left him with a small son to raise by himself. The boy wasn't three years old. She died of something called a milk leg. For the next ten years he raised his son alone.

"Your father was thirteen or fourteen years older than I. We got married, and a couple of years later you came along. It was right after that it happened. Somebody turned me in to the Feds—me and your Aunt Lucinda. But before they could come for us, we got a tip they knew everything, that we were here illegally, and so on. Your aunt immediately skipped the country. She made a beeline right to Vila Ruiva da Serra, vowing she'd never leave home again no matter what. As far as she was concerned, she had never set foot in America. But what could I do, married and with a brand–new baby? Your father and I talked about it. We agonized. Finally, it was decided that I had to turn myself in to the immigration officials. Good thing we did. They treated us fairly, your father and me. We were told that I had to leave the country for at least a year, and that if I did so I would then be allowed to come back—legally this time—as your father's wife and as the mother of an American child. They suggested that I go to Mexico or Canada, because they were the foreign countries closest to America. But your father decided against them. Rather than Mexico or Canada, we should go home. 'After all,' he explained, 'you can stay mainly with your family, and part of the time you can stay with my family, my father and mother, my brother and his wife. They can all get to know you. On both sides of the family, they'll have an opportunity to see the baby. That way time will go faster for you, and knowing you are safe with my family and your family, it will go faster for me, too.'

"And that's what happened. The sea voyage, though, was very long and the weather was bad. It was very crowded below deck. I thought we'd never get there." She hesitated, and then said, "I just remembered something funny. When we finally arrived in Lisbon—no, I mean Providence—and were told to line up to prepare for disembarking, we ended up way back in the line, an endless line that didn't seem to be moving at all. I was carrying you in my arms, of course, and you were getting heavier by the minute. But you were being good, just looking around, quietly, at everything in sight. You were perfectly happy, minding your business, until, that is, I pinched you—hard—and you began to bawl, first, and then to scream at the top of your lungs. It got everybody's attention, of course, and we were promptly called up to the front of the line. They went through my papers as quickly as they could. In two minutes we were out of there and on our way down the gangplank. You weren't much of a crier usually, but you were still sobbing when we set foot on the dock, where your father was waiting, smoking a cigarette—which didn't bother me a bit."

IRENE MARQUES

Irene Marques is a bilingual writer writing in English and Portuguese and an academic, holding a PhD in Comparative Literature and a Masters in both Comparative Literature and French Literature, all from the University of Toronto, as well as a Bachelor of Social Work from Ryerson University. She currently teaches in the African Studies Program at the University of Toronto and the Department of Languages, Literatures and Linguistics at York University and occasionally also at Ryerson University in the Department of English. In the past she has taught at the Ontario College of Art and Design University and also worked at the Centre for Addiction and Mental Health.

Marques is the author of three poetry collections in English—*Wearing Glasses of Water* (Mawenzi House, formerly TSAR Publications, 2007), *The Perfect Unravelling of the Spirit* (Mawenzi House, formerly TSAR Publications, 2012) and *The Circular Incantation: An Exercise in Loss and Findings* (Guernica Editions, 2013)—as well as the Portuguese language short story collection *Habitando na Metáfora do Tempo: Crónicas Desejadas* (Edium Editores, 2009) and the novel *My House is a Mansion* (Leaping Lion Books/York University, 2015). The novel *Uma Casa no Mundo* and the collection of short stories *Procurando Maravilhas* (both in Portuguese) are scheduled for publication in 2016. Her academic publications include the manuscripts *Transnational Discourses on Class, Gender and Cultural Identity* (Purdue University Press, 2011) and *Critical Approaches: The Works of Chin Ce, Volume 1* (Editor) (Handel Books, 2008) and numerous articles in international scholarly journals including *Research in African Literatures, African Identities* and *CLCWeb: Comparative Literature and Culture.*

The Making of Beautiful Stories

If I write down only an A then the story only exists in the
possibility of what could be—if I look at the A long enough
and whistle sounds of wisdom mingled with whispers of sorrows
emitted by old Portuguese widows, who have long ago lost their loving
men, then perhaps the story of the A will start being more
than a possible idea, or the awe of waiting, to become the
real harshness of those women with their black clothes
hanging down their twisted legs, tired monuments full of
varicose veins—caves concave

Dresses and dresses of black capes that sing long dark
fado songs that sound like howls of lost and very needy
madonnas—waiting and waiting for the day of redemption
when Jesus or his Father will come down and gently deliver
them from the pain of suffering by lifting them up to the
azures of the skies where the air dances with you and you
with it—like whirls of transcendental and pure evocations
—concave caves

And if I wait even longer and do other dances and
movements with that single and first letter of our long
alphabet, then I will be able to find more and more stories
—each letter emitting the cries of long lonely nights and
the noisy murmurs of rosaries going around and around,
encircling the fingers of the widows even when they
lay down in bed at night and ought to enter the land of
oblivion

Each letter speaking to the other like sisters of the
same sorrow, nuns of the same loveless nights, desolate
monastery, because widows are single, single women who
must remain in the cell until the rest of their days—the old
ladies of eternity who must tell their breasts and the pulse
pulsating between their legs to calm, calm down, because
sins will take us to the inferno flames where we will forever
burn and pain

And when I arrive at the end of the line that the Z is,
I know in my bones how loneliness is forged through
night after night of incantations intimated by the priest
—incantations told to women about what they really are

and must always remain—yes because God never, never forgives—and then we die exhausted by the weight of the days that have left nothing on our scant bodies—nothing to anchor upon, except the imaginings of the perfect return

The Blood of Goats

Adsamo in a painting
Adsamo: the little place where I was born
And spent sublime times with goats of all colors, horns of all sizes
Hard rocks, twisted in circles and semi–moons that created light and
        shadow
And served to ward off mean males in heat looking for undue trouble

They are selling their blood now in the laboratories of California
The beautiful animals which have so much spirit and grace
Sisters of the gazelles, neck elevated and eyes searching and aware
Kept in a cage to breed blood for you and I
Injected with the diseases that we, you and I, do not want

They stand by the gate, paws on the net, eyes staring from the holes
Legs broken, ridden with anemia, tumors in the belly and
        bronchopneumonia
We pass by every day, we buy coffee at Starbucks and Acqua Cologne to
        save the children
But fail to see the link between our lifestyle and theirs
And in fact feel good that we are doing our part
Each bottle of Cologne provides 10 liters of clean water for the children
And a pound of eco–ethical coffee, non–critical
Pays the salary of a Guatemalan for a month

Give me a "grande" please? Do they know that a "grande" is a large and
        not a regular?
They use Latin to gain influence and regain the empire of the old
When there were less mugs and stores and ripped jeans and people seemed
        to be more emotional—say hello and look you in the eye, really in
        the eye, staying there for a while

We go on through the day, and in moments of insight, and we have many
Because we are not dead yet—in those moments
We want to scream at our boss, tell her to fuck off, and run out the door
To go and do something, really something
But can we? Isn't the beast in every cup we drink, in every thought we
        think?
If only we could sleep quietly and then dream—an empty Marxist marvel
A real dream of a real world where everything made sense

Adsamo in a painting

Frozen in a nest of sparrows, eggs round and equal
Life bulging inside
Like when I was young and beautiful
And perfect
And everything was and would be

Taking Photographs

I take shots of crickets that live in their holes, of the grasshoppers that stutter trying to fly great distances in windy days

I take shots of the spaces between my fingers and the back of my bone—trying to find the memory of my pain because if I see it I can then paint upon it—imprint roses and breeding bread, roses and slow incantations and then I will make anew what I always knew I could and would be after some concentrated exercise, the type that requires shallow breathing and stillness of the body—the final touch–up of the great media artist—fading away the bleeding bubbling particles that damage the perfect

I take shots of my back inverting my body to immeasurable somersaults and then I see the ribs that make me and align my shadow with the altitude of life

I take the camera even further down, down of myself and I enter the moist moss down below—becoming acquainted with Pluto—I converse with him because he is in a good mood, optimistic of the moment—he guides me through the tortuous channels that life is before becoming life in the pulsating of the upstairs window

I allow him to give me his hand, moistened from the dew down there, because at first I am afraid of losing who I am in the muddy humid overland of the below—and then, after his patience teaches me the way, I walk freely and motivated, alone, unafraid to remember where I come from and where I will return, after I live the life I am when I am not filming this film taking this photograph

I swim with such dexterity now that all the underworld seems to be a very familiar site—an intimate one even, as if my blood remembers the humidity that I have always been by the power of some incantation that stayed alive in the surface of my skin, crawling upon me like a quilt of the transcendent—travelling certain and concrete to the river vessels of my brain—the lymph nodes that keep me alert to the trans–nationality of my being, the splendorous Hollywood of my long time career

I emerge from there returning to the upper levels of existence and then I take more shots to add to my already complex long line of *películas*

I take shots of the dark spaces of the moon, of the shadows of the white roses and the underlying movements of the light blue hydrangeas, of the bridges underneath the rail train capturing the noises of the screeching wheels when they pass above me, or the perfect moving silence that appears in the eyes of the passengers of life who sit there unaware of their awareness, being conducted by the great conductor of this line

I also take presence of the saints at the church—of Saint Laura and Saint Amelia who lie side by side in their perfect eternal poses, decorations to the altar—Madonnas of all time, I touch their faces and see the effigies that they have become to preserve beauty and the virginity of being—the Buddhas of the orient in the adoration that is required by thee

I film the Day of All Saints—by a miracle of unseen force my camera imprints the impressions of the many that have moved to the crust below where I have just been, as photographed above—their transparent presences transpire through the magnetic field that is my camera, a somersault to the visible invisible

I cross the altar slowly, like a butterfly priest incanting the eternal mass evoked and invoked over and over through the vast lazy centuries, and I take shots of me, of you, of the baptisms that have been performed since Christianity became a religion to be followed by believers, of the brides who have swept that cold clear floor that is the altar with their long beautiful white dresses trying to rescue the mime of the true truth, like innocent children born to execute the marvellous and make things forever lasting

I shoot the arias and the nuptial marches and that secret moment when the body and the blood of Christ enter my mouth and yours making us cannibals of the divine

I then shoot the voice of the priest of the last rites performing the *última missa* for my darling friend Isabel who died last fall in that sullen November—I capture his breath as he incants the words that will allow her to escape the devil's paws and enter the golden gate of heaven or the garden, the garden of O—I approach the casket and I see her, Isabel, in a white dress, dressed for the gods, I dreamed of her like that, *noiva em branco para Deus*, even he needs a virgin to feast upon, I dreamed of her like that the night before she died—I see roses and roses upon her frail body eaten by the leech of cancer—I see roses and roses upon her frail body incanting it before it forever goes—cell by cell— bone by bone—even the marrow— that sacred humidity of life where everything lies

I go deeper inwards and I photograph her entrails still intact, at least to the visible eye, and then I wait longer and I see the primal worms at work attacking her core, and then I stay there staring in concentration with my lens and I see her form going and going, disintegrating the inner walls and bursting into the white satin and fleecy clouds of the house she was put in after her heart said: "No, no more, no more, because death is my final destination, my ultimate *abraço*!"—and then ahead, much ahead, my lens captures the other forms, the ones that she will become because becoming is her fortune and mine too—as a final act of this film my camera sinks down below again and SHE becomes spattered, on the walls—portrait of the unswayable—my beloved friend Isabel

I still shoot the word INRI on the cross holding that famous man who died for all of us of this religion—I fix my lens attentively on it staying there for longer than I remember how to tell you and then the world under inspection transmutes to a long vast poem that I cannot contain in me, for it evades the small iris of my filming vision—but then I move slightly so that I can get the perfect angle and my vision field becomes all the poetry that is possible to shoot under the canvas of being

I take shots and shots because my world and yours is everywhere I turn
I am a camera all over my body, filming me, filming you and all the spaces that lay between us

ANTONIO LADEIRA

António Ladeira was born in Portugal in 1969. He lived in the US since 1993. He is currently Associate Professor of Portuguese at Texas Tech University where he serves as the director of the Portuguese program. He has had teaching appointments at Middlebury College and Yale University. He holds a *licenciatura* in Portuguese Studies from the Universidade Nova de Lisboa and a PhD in Hispanic Languages and Literatures from the University of California in Santa Barbara. He has published, in Portugal, four books of his own poetry. In 2010 a poem of his was included in *Resumo*, a selection of the best poetry published in Portugal (FNAC). His poems have appeared in *Colóquio–Letras* (Lisbon), *Jornal de Letras* (Lisbon), *Prairie Schooner* (University of Nebraska) and in the *Interdisciplinary Journal of Portuguese Diaspora Studies*, where he serves as a member of the editorial board. In 2001 he organized an international conference on Portuguese–American Literature at Yale University titled "Portuguese–American Literature: the first One hundred Years." In 2005 he was co–editor of a dossier on Portuguese–American literature in the academic Journal *Hispania*. As guest editor, he has prepared a volume on Portuguese–American literature for *Gávea–Brown* (Brown University, 2012–2013).

Outra mentira

Esta rua onde vivemos
vai desaparecer.

Esta cidade que nos recorda ainda
vai desaparecer.

Vai desaparecer a canção que agora escutas
ao balcão de um bar, barricado.

A convulsão do mar
a sua tosse infinita de fumador inveterado
vale hoje tanto como uma das promessas frementes
com que vencíamos a noite.

Sim, a nossa vida terminou.

Resta acompanhar com o olhar esta mulher velha
que sobe a custo a rua empedrada
depois de comprar dois pães na loja.

Vê–la limpar lentamente os pés no tapete
entrar na casa humilde
fechando atrás de si, com estrondo,
a porta.

Não somos aqueles adolescentes
que acordavam de manhã
cheios de planos;
e às vezes caminhavam juntos
por ruas perigosas e estreitas.

Ia dizer: não somos aqueles adolescentes
que riam perdidamente
sem razões.

Mas seria outra mentira.

Perder tempo

Sempre perdi tempo.

Enquanto os amigos publicavam livros sucessivos
ganhavam prémios
enlouqueciam respeitavelmente
enriqueciam pelos seus próprios méritos
(não os que tinham publicado livros!)
e outros faziam construir —os que estudaram arquitectura—
casas magníficas como as que vemos em revistas,
igrejas altíssimas e até, suponho,
catedrais
eu ficava a fumar horas a fio, no escuro,
com a televisao sintonizada no programa mais imbecil que encontrava
(porque o mais imbecil dos programas era mais inteligente
do que os programas inteligentes!).

Com ar sonhador, mastigando o meu almoço,
pensava em mulheres inacessíveis
em carros último modelo que me faziam sorrir num sobressalto
apesar de saber —ou talvez por isso—
que estariam sempre além do meu alcance;
em empregos fabulosos onde se ia de escadas rolantes
do primeiro ao segundo andar
e onde sapatos, muito engraxados,
pisavam delicamente um chão de mármore
como a superfície polida de um lago
onde toda gente se cumprimentava
com correcção e cortesia
dizendo, jovialmente, 'muito bom dia!'
ou 'ontem lá voltei tarde da festa!'

No meu sofá verde, de noite,
tecia estes febris pensamentos, sem ordem nem propósito,
tão inócuos, enervantes, familiares
e, ao mesmo tempo, tão estranhamente tranquilizadores.

É verdade,
nunca tive ambições nem por cá passaram planos;
Mas fui tão feliz.

Na livraria

Lembro–me do tempo em que
numa mesa de café, num autocarro
numa sala de espera, na fila de uma livraria
me apercebia imediatamente do desejo
no olhar de uma rapariga.

Aquele olhar baixo, disfarçadamente ferido de desejo
o corpo interiormente contorcido de curiosidade erótica
o sorriso subtil que por vezes libertava uma chispa maligna
o lábio escarlate mordido escandalosamente, irreprimivelmente,
como a última onda que quebra numa praia
vedada a turistas por haver perigo de derrocada;
ou numa praia em cujo parque de estacionamento
fosse impossível encontrar o carro que lá tivéssemos deixado
ou, caso se encontrasse, não se pudesse entrar nele
por ter uma temperatura superior à do planeta Mercúrio
por ter estado à torreira do sol
a tarde toda.

Hoje, depois de partir bruscamente e olhar uma última vez para trás
não sei se o seu olhar é propositadamente displicente
para que me decida de uma vez a seguí–la pelas ruas
como teria feito o adolescente insensato que fui
que saberia convencê–la e, sobretudo, convencer–se a si mesmo
de que não poderia viver mais um dia
sem o seu número de telefone;
ou se, pelo contrário,
o enfado fingido é, na verdade,
o mais real dos enfados.

Na mesa da livraria, à minha frente,
bocejas enquanto finges folhear uma revista
ou de actrizes de cinema que perderam peso
ou de operações plásticas com resultados catastróficos.

Olhas para o relógio a cada dois minutos
com a mal disfarçada impaciência com que arrumas a revista na estante
o que pode significar o que gostaria tanto que significasse
—ou o que de facto significa.

Preparas–te para sair
e eu volto ao meu jornal;
é a vida.

Talvez à beira de um lago

Estou em casa.

Estou na sua temperatura.

Na cozinha, como quase sempre a esta hora da madrugada.

Rodeado dos meus amigos pratos, dos garfos meus amigos.

Dos copos que, ocasionalmente, parecem tilintar, malévolos.

Os ângulos mais embotados das facas oxidadas
esperam pacientemente no interior das gavetas.

Não têm pressa, têm tempo.

É então que as conversas antigas recomeçam,
a princípio são vozes de quem está à mesa,
talvez um dia festivo
ou a preparação de uma viagem.

Depois, tornam—se íntimas, intermináveis,
como quando se está para adormecer.

Gente que um dia conheci e que desapareceu.

Que reconhecerei um dia, talvez distraído,
talvez à beira de um lago.

ALYSE KNORR

Alyse Knorr is the author of *Copper Mother* (Switchback Books), <u>Annotated Glass</u> (Furniture Press Books), *Epithalamia* (Horse Less Press), and *Alternates* (dancing girl press). She received her MFA from George Mason University. She teaches at the University of Alaska Anchorage and serves as a founding co-editor of Gazing Grain Press. Her work has appeared or is forthcoming in *Drunken Boat, Puerto Del Sol, RHINO, The Minnesota Review*, and *The Southern Poetry Anthology*. Knorr teaches English at the University of Alaska Anchorage. Visit her at www.alyseknorr.com.

The Great Inheritance

My great–grandmother Eutilia, brought across the ocean to put an end
to her love affairs. In a tenement kitchen in East Providence,
she sits with my mother, age 3, drinking tea and speaking with her
in Portuguese—*você está com fome, fala de novo*—
a language my mother will forget entirely, save the names
of the soups and biscuits—*caldo verde, caldeirada, queijada*—
that she will try, and fail, to cook correctly as a grown woman,
as my mother, decades later: always something wrong,
some ingredient missing she can't remember the name of,
and no relatives left to call and ask, though even if she were still
alive, and even if she could speak English, would Eutilia recognize this
        woman
on the other line, using words like "y'all" and not sounding at all
like the three–year–old babbling nonsense words at the breakfast table,
trying out the Portuguese sounds for her grandmother, both of them
        laughing
(she laughs for no one else), both with the same green eyes—
the eyes of the witch, the old ones say, the eyes of the millionaire,
the eyes of the woman who left behind a fortune
no one since has ever dared claim.

Fazenda

If I had known her then, had I been born
of another woman's blood and not hers,
in time to see her walking the fields with her linen
dress and the dark hair of all of my mothers,
green eyes squinting through rain at the men,
yelling at them to finish the row, 20 seeds per hole—
half will die naturally—yelling at the men and patting
the earth down smooth with her rough palms and
mouthing a prayer over it, or a spell—a gesture
the men will see and note in whispers later, at the tavern—
returning home later to a woman
and putting her hands on that woman's hips;
breathing the living coffee onto her lips.

RICHARD SIMAS

Richard Simas is a free–lance writer with a background in literature, music, and the performing arts. He contributes regularly to contemporary art and literary reviews and has published in Europe and in North America, including the Journey Prize anthology. He is also a winner of a Fiddlehead Fiction Prize. His short fiction is included in *Memória*, an anthology of Portuguese Canadian writers. He contributes regularly to Toronto's *Musicworks* magazine. Thanks to an award from Portugal's Camões Institute in 2011, he attended the Disquiet International Literature program in Lisbon and in 2012 published a series of interviews with 4 contemporary Portuguese writers. He has published a series of essays about exploring Portuguese immigrant heritage and the notion of (re)learning Portuguese from a diaspora perspective. In Montreal, Simas founded Théâtre La Chapelle, an interdisciplinary performing centre dedicated to multidisciplinary experimentation. He currently performs with a nine–member street band named Valody whose New Music–Spoken word performance based on Fernando Pessoa's *Book of Disquiet* premiered at the Open Ears festival in Kitchener Ontario. He co–organizes the *Café com letras lusophone* literature readings in Montreal.

Interrogations: Narrating Luso Diaspora, Fact or Ficção?[1]

> *The past is a country from which we have all emigrated ... its loss is part of our common humanity.*
> *Salman Rushdie*

Writing about Luso–diaspora is a project of inventing home by unlocking a door, inserting questions in a keyhole, turning the bolt, and lifting the latch. My fingers twist the doorknob open to discover tales of arrival, departure, and dislocation: true stories, lies, reports, speculations, gossip, myths, memories, and possibilities. Salman Rushdie penned the perspective succinctly in his essay "Imaginary Homelands:" "If we do look back...we will not be capable of reclaiming precisely the thing that was lost; ...we will, in short, create fictions, not actual cities or villages, but invisible ones, imaginary homelands..."[2]

Where is Truth? In Fact or Ficção?

For me, the borders between fact and fiction immediately appeared tentative when I became interested in Luso–diaspora. It was not at all clear whether I was considering facts from my distant, third–generation California–Azorean immigrant heritage or riding a wave of exotic, ethnic exploration.

I explored the Luso community in Montreal, attending *festas*, and began reading Azorean literature and North American Luso writers. I tried to understand why immigrants from the continent said, "Oh, they are Azoreans" and the Azoreans said, "We are Portuguese." I sensed echoes, shadows, and the long fingers of memory beckoning, but I had very few facts to work with because no one chronicled our ancestors' voyage or could even say exactly where we were from. We were generic not specific, but invention is one way to reverse such a situation.

While parading with a Portuguese marching band in the Fall River *festas* and

---

[1] Adapted from a text presented during the Exploring Luso–North American Diaspora, Nem Cá Nem Lá, Mas Também–Neither Here Nor There Yet Both.
[2] Salman Rushdie, Imaginary Homelands. Granta Books, 1991. P. 10

singing with a folk group at a *Matança do Porco* in Montreal's Casa dos Açores, I couldn't say if my experiences resonated as facts of real heritage or intriguing voyeurisms. Something beyond fabulous fictions whispered, 'come closer.'

Assuming roles as both 'outside' observer and returning prodigal son, divided yet again, I suspected that being fragmented and scattered was in itself a "home" –a fertile, creative place to reflect on one's imperfection, impurity, and incoherence. Rushdie's image for this condition is that of an unearthed pottery shard that immediately provokes wonder and speculation about missing pieces. I pocketed my find and dug deeper.

Narrative is movement from one place to another, even in such an immobile voyage as Pessoa's *Book of Disquiet*, that metaphysical solo–dance with the universe. For me, writing a diaspora narrative required traveling where distinctions between fact and fiction revealed themselves as secondary. Even if it had been my intention to be exact, so many facts are absent, contradictory, boring, disputed, unsatisfactory, forgotten, and unknowable that such an enterprise would be impossible. Memory is suspect when it must testify in court, but adrift in this vast diaspora sea, metaphor, speculation, and intuition prove themselves alluring and useful evidence. Fictive buoys float me closer to an essence of the past.

Reclaiming What Language?

Language is useful in interrogations, and the one I imagine losing happens to be Portuguese. I heard only a handful of Portuguese words while growing up. Old people whispered foreign words when sharing secrets or hiding comments unsuitable to a child's ears. Nothing could be more attractive. Not far from Steinbeck's Tortilla Flats, on the Central Coast of California, Portuguese was not an embarrassing immigrant language for us nor did it appear to have any practical usage. Looking back, the social situation appeared fluid. Many people were relatively recent immigrants and everyone managed in English, even if it was imperfect: Mexicans, Japanese, Swiss–Italians, Portuguese, and Koreans. In a place where we learned Spanish as a second language, accents and inventive language usage were common.

Like a true surfer gringo kid, I chattered the few Portuguese words I knew with only vague notions about what they meant. No one thought it important to teach me more. Still, in the mouths of the old people, I liked hearing hybrid words slide between two languages, vowels oddly extended and tacked to the tail of an English word, a scrap of song drifting a sentence away in a voice not wanting to end. The differences intrigued rather than embarrassed me, probably because we didn't have to struggle to prove we were like everyone else. I thought we were. What a shock then when, already an adult, I was asked, "Is English your first language?"

I thought it was my only language, but maybe it was "secondary" and according to a graduate writing teacher, imperfect. The first seed of doubt was planted long ago: perhaps another language was hiding inside of me, ducking behind slightly unstable English syntax and waiting to be mouthed. Even more enchanting, perhaps this "other" tongue belonged to me, was part of my distant diaspora DNA, and destined to appear, much like genetic details.

Great desires emerge from doubt: I wanted to know what it was like for those "old people" to have crammed new, foreign, English words into their mouths. What new impulse did their souls accommodate when the word "heart" replaced *coração*, "tired" instead of *cansado*, and *trabalho* became "work?" The only way to know was to reverse a voyage, return their words to me, because perhaps it was my language and a key to open the door.

Desire. *Desejo.* Hope. *Esperança. Eu esperava* that if I blew onto this new, old language it would flare to life, bright, powerful, particular. *Eu esperava* that it would reunite the one who left with the one who stayed behind. It was the last chance *a última ocasião* before the old words expired, crawling into a cold grave next to the elders' bones.

Three generations later, I hoped shadows *as sombras* of the old, new language remained, defying time and geography, an indelible color *uma cor indelével*, refusing to disappear, no matter how unused and ignored. But that was fiction not fact. In truth, nothing remained or perhaps ever existed. I would have to start over again to learn a language that I imagined was already mine.

I stubbornly breathed onto dying words, awaiting a response. When I finally spoke in Portuguese, confusion emerged, fragments *fragmentos* of utterances as if diaspora terrorists had exploded a Tower of Babel to punish my arrogance, releasing a torrent of unidentifiable words *palavras não–identificáveis*, multiple errors of the masculine and feminine genders, tangles of verb tenses, and misused articles and prepositions. Garbled sounds and squawks resulted, more fitting to migrating birds than to a prodigal Luso–son knocking at the door and begging for his inheritance.

What to do? Perhaps there was an error. Secrets and skeletons lurking in the family closet? Maybe I mistook the appropriate diaspora door and should have knocked elsewhere: Orientals, Scandinavians, Latvians, Jews, or the mysterious Basques. Oh why didn't the ancestors teach me their language? Did they instead bequeath me a challenge in order to build character? Why can't I conjure their speech back to life inside me? Why am I one of Rushdie's unearthed pottery shards, a fragment missing from something bigger and broken? *Amor Fati*, Nietzsche advices, borrowing from Marcus Aurelius. "Love fate." Accept your destiny. Whatever happens to you is good, including suffering and loss.

If anything, I am a typically practical North American. I bought an English–Portuguese/Portuguese–English dictionary. I attempted to read *Os Lusíads* in Portuguese then exchanged the copy for an English version. I tried reading João de Melo in English, French, and Portuguese and failed in all three languages, though it was a wonderful adventure. Perhaps my people were not Azoreans after all.

My dictionary broke in half from overuse, unevenly, the Portuguese portion smaller than the English, suggesting a significant detail about geography. I bought a "Portuguese–only" dictionary, declaring my liberation from translation and wandered deeper into pure Luso territory with no safety–belt. *Traduzir: levar de um lugar ao outro lugar*, carry from one place to another. *Agora, tenho dois idiomas, os dois imperfeitos.*

Am I Luso Enough?

From things about to disappear I turn away in time. To watch them out of sight, no, I can't do it. –Samuel Beckett, 'Molloy'.[3]

Late at night, I worry about this "Luso–enough" question, whether I fit, am a fake *fingidor*, or if this is all another wild–goose chase and useless enterprise. What emerged from shadows could as easily disappear into them again. All illusion. I fear expulsion from a diaspora clan of which I am only a tentative member. I demand proof then wonder, in this awkward waltz between *me* and *us*, if I really want to belong. Which part of me, if any, is Luso: the doubter, the optimist, the sentimentalist, the tinkerer, the wanderer, or the one who loves a smoky barbecue fire? The *mim* that always cuts a piece of flesh when repairing something leaving a bloodstain to mark his presence? Is this my Luso–ness? *Como poderia o saber?*

I am afraid the mask *mascara* will fall that allows me to explore this other me and I will have to abandon believing that what truth there is lies in looking and finally very little separates fact from fiction. I take a deep breath in this moment when the bird flies to the ledge of an open window, peeks in, settles its wings, sings, and later moves on.

Why interrogate diaspora shadows when reality is exactly what hopeful ancestors dreamed of for their clan: a better, North American life. In their voyage and dream, they found their terra firma. *Parabéns!* For them, California in the prosperous twentieth century was a good place and time to begin again. *Amor Fati!* Love your destiny!

Which interrogation will explain why these Luso ghosts have stepped forth from the corners of a distant home? What is their message, and what do I have to do to hear it? Possibly I have misunderstood, because language, no matter how much you work it, remains an approximation. Oracles speak to me in Part–Portuguese with island accents from Pico and Terceira. I understand, "Hurry, you have to know what is inside before there is nothing left. Before we disappear! *Depressa!*" Voices and the power of poems seduce me, so I listen.

Concretely? Can laboratory tests determine if I am Luso enough? How long do I have to wear my Portuguese marching band uniform to prove it? Do I

---

[3] Beckett, Samuel, Molloy. Grove Press, 1955.

have to read Vitorino Nemésio and love Eça de Queiros? Surely drugs can be purchased to increase my Luso–ness.

A hundred years later, an immigrant son should be thoroughly transformed and free from the past. But we are never free. Perhaps the fate Nietzsche proposes to embrace implies completing the dream of someone before me, closing the diaspora circle of a hungry sharecropper from Pico by an educated new world professional. Still, I resist shutting the open window, finishing the story. Perhaps the bird will enter the room and not be able to escape.

As many of these tales exist as there are people at a party, and everyone has one to tell. It is stories' nature to continue in circles. Or they are scattered bits like Chinese pick–up sticks carefully retrieved one at a time until all are gathered in your hand. A story is a storm blowing past chaotically and also a carefully traced line, barely wavering from start to finish like a desert freeway.

Mine is a tangled ball of string, slowly unravelling to join the parts of a scattered self. It is a thread that fingers follow blindly across an unknown territory in search of home, wherever that might be. It is easy to lose a trail in someone else's dream.

Home. *Mas Também*. Veins open to hear blood pulsing beyond reasoning: masks, hopes, costumes, tongues. Interrogations. Perhaps this beat is Luso enough, *Luso–filho*, and my discovery of it connects me to a vaster world *um mundo mais vasto.*

ANTHONY BARCELLOS

Anthony Barcellos grew up speaking Portuguese on his grandfather's dairy farm in California's great Central Valley. His experiences inspired his debut novel, *Land of Milk and Money* (2012, Tagus Press). Barcellos currently resides in Davis, California, and is a senior faculty member of the mathematics department of American River College in Sacramento. While a teaching assistant at UC Davis, he received both the departmental and campus awards for teaching excellence; in addition, the students at ARC selected him for a Teacher of the Year award. Barcellos is coauthor (with Sherman K. Stein) of *Calculus and Analytic Geometry* (McGraw–Hill, 1992) and received expository writing awards for "The Fractal Geometry of Mandelbrot" (College Math Journal). He has worked as a science journalist (*Albuquerque Journal*), legislative assistant (California State Senate), and program officer (California State Treasurer's Office). He holds a Ph.D. from the UC Davis School of Education and is also an alumnus of Porterville College, Caltech, and Fresno State.

The Voyage to Brazil: May 1865

The shriek of splintering wood shattered the afternoon stillness. The passengers and crew of the *Bella Flor* felt the deck shudder momentarily under their feet before the vessel settled back to a passive rolling with the Atlantic's swells. Smoke continued to pour from the steamship's stacks, but the paddle wheels were motionless and so essentially was the *Bella Flor*. Passengers were making the sign of the cross and some of the women began to weep.

António Gabriel "*Mestre*" Francisco turned to his wife Diolinda.

"Now they'll have to listen to me," he told her.

Diolinda squeezed his hand.

"I pray that they will," she said. "The children and I will go below and say the rosary."

"*Mãe!*" protested ten–year–old Candido Paulo, their eldest child. He didn't want to squeeze back into their lower–deck cabin with his mother and his three siblings, but his mother was firm as she herded her brood toward the narrow stairs that would take them below decks.

António went looking for a crew member.

The captain and the executive officer of the *Bella Flor* were conferring on the bridge when a deckhand appeared.

"Message for the captain, sir!" he said.

"Yes?" said the captain.

"It's another message from the passenger named Francisco, sir. He's volunteering his services again, sir."

"'Again'?" echoed the captain. "He's done this before?"

"Begging your pardon, sir," said the executive officer. "This passenger claims to be a skilled craftsman and has been putting himself forward since the initial incident. He's an islander we picked up during our stop in the Azores. I informed him that the crew would handle the matter and thanked him for his concern. It didn't seem necessary to bring it to your attention, sir."

"Ordinarily I would say you did the right thing, Number One," said the captain. "Unfortunately, however, it appears that the crew is *not* handling the matter."

The captain turned back to the deckhand.

"Please fetch this man—did you say 'Francisco'?—fetch *Senhor* Francisco to the bridge. I wish to confer with our *soi–disant* skilled craftsman. Let's see if he is what he says. The Lord knows we need one right now."

*

The crewman led António Francisco onto the bridge.

"Sir! Here is *Senhor* Francisco."

"Thank you," said the captain. "You may go."

He regarded his passenger, a wiry man in his mid–thirties with dark wavy hair and dark eyes. The executive officer had said that Francisco was an Azorean, and he looked the part.

António Francisco looked back at the captain, bemused by the uniform that sported as much elaborate tailoring as would suit the admiral of a fleet. He kept his face expressionless. Perhaps the outfit was not the captain's fault. Perhaps the shipping company that owned the *Bella Flor* thought to impress their passengers with comic–opera uniforms for their senior officers.

"*Senhor* Francisco," said the captain, "I regret to share with you the information that our vessel is in difficulty. Since you have repeatedly volunteered to help us resolve the problem, I presume you have discerned the difficulty for yourself."

"Yes, *capitão*," António replied. "We have been adrift for ten days now. All of us heard the noise of the accident. The same noise followed the repairs. We heard much splintering of wood, no? I think maybe you have wooden gears with many broken teeth in your drive train, yes?"

"You judge correctly, *Senhor* Francisco. Furthermore, ship's stores are able to supply material sufficient for only one more repair effort. As you may appreciate, splintered wood is impossible to salvage and the next attempt must succeed. Either that, or we are adrift until good fortune miraculously brings another vessel alongside to rescue us. We are already overdue at Rio de Janeiro, but we cannot expect anyone to be actively looking for us yet. What gives you the confidence to put yourself forward as someone who can repair our vessel? Are you some kind of nautical engineer?"

"No, sir," replied António, "but I know materials and machinery— especially wood. I am known on Terceira as '*mestre*' or 'master' for my skills, which I am putting at your service."

"Very well, *Mestre* Francisco," said the captain. "I will have you shown to the paddle wheels, where you will have full access to their enclosure, including the gears, drive train, and the paddle wheels themselves. My executive officer will escort you. The XO will report back to me with your plans, however, before you are to do anything, which is contingent on my prior approval. Is that understood?"

António gave the captain a small bow.

"Yes, *capitão*. You are most generous, *senhor*. I will discuss matters with your executive officer and will wait for your command."

The captain turned to his executive officer.

"Take him below, Number One."

*

"Here we are, *senhor*," said the executive officer of the *Bella Flor*. He pulled a hatch aside, admitting them into an enclosed space amidships. It was a wide compartment that opened on either side to the paddle wheel enclosures. From below came the sounds of the water lapping against the ship and the motionless paddles. The men could hear a quiet creaking as the ship rocked gently with the Atlantic's low swells.

"We are next to the engine room," continued the officer. "These shafts and gears can be engaged to propel the ship forward, to let the paddles idle in free–wheeling mode, or to back water and slow or reverse the ship's motion. It is a British design that was adapted and implemented in a shipyard in Oporto when the *Flor* was refitted fifteen—maybe sixteen— years ago."

António Francisco cast his eyes over the gears, gap–toothed with their shattered wooden cogs. As much as he liked wood as a building material, António questioned the wisdom of making it the principal component of the ship's drive mechanism. Steel was used sparingly and economically to reinforce the gears. No doubt the owners of the *Bella Flor* had saved money, but now their cargo and their passengers would be late in making port at Rio. If they arrived at all.

The executive officer watched António closely as the islander peered through the mechanism and examined the gears from different angles, occasionally rocking them back and forth. He waited patiently until António finished his inspection and stood up straight, turning toward the officer.

"What do you think, *Mestre* Francisco? Can you fix it?"

"Of course," said António. "I can fix it. I will get my tools. Please to have your men remove the broken cogs. I will be able to use some of the fragments. Also have them bring up the wood remaining in ship's stores and lay the pieces out for my inspection. I will begin immediately."

"Very well," said the executive officer. "Once I report to the captain, I am certain it will be as you say, *mestre*."

*

Never before in his young life had Candido Paulo Francisco worn shoes for so many consecutive days. At his mother's insistence, all of the children were in boots or shoes and bundled up with multiple layers of clothing. All the rest of their worldly belongings were packed in two steamer trunks in the ship's hold.

Now at last Candido Paulo had a good excuse to set his shoes aside and employ all twenty digits in his father's service. He sat on the deck with a length of cargo net stretched between his toes while his nimble fingers wove cord through the interstices to tighten the mesh. Generations of Candido Paulo's forebears had similarly worked on their fishing nets on the beaches of Portugal and its islands. The boy was fashioning a mesh bag for his father's use in the ship's drive chamber. António would need something in which to hold some tools and materials while he worked. When nothing more suitable came to hand, he had set his son working on a swatch of cargo net. The boy was pleased to do it and it would serve.

His father was nearby, the remaining lumber from the ship's stores arrayed about him. António sorted out the short wooden blocks intended for use as gear cogs and grouped them into sets for the gears that drove the ship's paddle wheels. He also had a collection of splintered wood consisting of the remains of the shattered cogs that the crew had pried out of the shorn gears. He picked out some of the more substantial chunks and went to work with his one–handed splitting maul, reducing them to a pile of sharp–edged shims of varying lengths and thicknesses.

Candido Paulo brought his handiwork over to his father. He had added the finishing touch of weaving a cord through the perimeter of the netting for use as a drawstring. António placed a stack of his newly created shims in the center of Candido Paulo's tightly–woven mesh, added the maul, and pulled on the drawstring, gathering up the net into a bundle. He fastened it to his belt with a short length of cord. The bundle dangled at his side from his waist to his knee.

"*Bem feito*," he told his son. *Well done.* The boy beamed.

"Put your shoes back on, son. There are splinters everywhere."

Candido Paulo sat down on the deck and reluctantly did as he was told. He brightened, however, at his father's next words.

"Come with me. You will be my helper, yes?"

"*Sim, senhor!*" Yes, sir!

*

The cylindrical steel power shaft had been decoupled from the drive mechanism of the paddle wheels. The shaft would start turning if the engineer in the boiler room engaged the clutch, but paddle–wheel gears would remain idle while António was working on them. The wooden gears were banded with steel reinforcements, gaping holes in their circumferences showing where their broken teeth had been extracted. The whole assembly looked like a scaled–up version of a clock's inner workings.

António shrugged off his suspenders and unbuttoned his shirt. He pulled it off and handed the shirt to Candido Paulo. He pushed the sleeves of his long–johns back to his elbows and pulled the suspenders back over his shoulders.

"Look at this, boy."

António slapped his hand several times against the gear that would normally have engaged the power shaft. It spun freely and rapidly on its axle.

Candido Paulo was standing to one side. From his vantage point, the empty holes for the gear's teeth began to blur together, making a darker band in the middle of the gear's circumference. The dark band wobbled back and forth with a slow oscillation that was almost hypnotic. The boy peered at it, wondering what he was supposed to see. Then his eyes widened and he jerked his head, looking toward his father.

"It's moving, *Pai*," he said. "I mean, the holes. They wobble back and forth."

"Exactly," said António. "It's out of true. The wooden gears on this old tub are warped with age and use. You see them wandering—just a bit—from left to right and back again as the wheel spins. I suspect it is the same for all of the gears. If they are all out of true, there will be a twisting of the teeth when they mesh and try to turn. If it's too much, they break. That is what I must repair."

"How will you do that, *Pai*? You can't work the steel parts, can you?"

"No, son. But I can remount the cogs and adjust them so that they are nevertheless in alignment."

António patted the mesh bag dangling from his hip.

"My tools are here. These tools and a good eye will suffice. Go fetch the first set of replacement cogs. We will fix this first one together as a test. Then I will climb inside and see what I can do with the others."

*

It took almost two days. António lived among the gears for the entire time. He would unship each gear in its turn so that it revolved freely. One by one he replaced the missing cogs and spun the gear to check the alignment. Periodically he reached into his bag for a thin wooden shim. He'd place it carefully next to an errant cog and use the flat end of his maul to tap it into place. Then another spin to see if the alignment had been corrected. More tapping, if necessary. More spinning. When the spinning wooden cogs blurred into a steady and unwavering band under his watchful eye, he'd remount the gear and move on to the next. Candido Paulo hovered nearby, fetching materials as his father requested them. Crewmen brought lanterns as the day gave way to evening.

A plank and some ropes provided a crude scaffold that enabled António to dangle in the open spaces above the water as he worked the ends of the drive train closer to the paddle wheels. Diolinda periodically appeared with a basket of provisions, which Candido Paulo would deliver to his father, who ate sparingly.

António's body was trembling with exhaustion and his eyes were rimmed with red when he climbed out of the congeries of gears and reconnected the power shaft. Anxious crewmen were watching. The executive officer was among them.

"I am done, *senhor*," said António. "Please to tell the captain."

Candido Paulo gave his father the shirt he had discarded the day before. Instead of putting it back on, António wiped his face with it, the thick fabric rasping against his growth of beard.

They waited, sitting on the deck, looking at the power shaft from the engine room. Most of the loitering crewmen were gone, presumably reporting to their posts. A couple remained, though, their eyes on the drive mechanism.

A whistle sounded. It sounded again. A loud mechanical clash was heard from below decks. The engineer had engaged the clutch.

The shaft was slowly beginning to turn, applying power to the gears. The gears were moving. António appeared relaxed, but Candido Paulo was holding his breath.

They heard the slapping of the paddle wheels against the water. The *Bella Flor* was starting to move. Candido Paulo started to breathe again.

Father and son looked at each other and smiled.

DIANA RAMOS FIRESTONE

Diana Ramos Firestone, a Portuguese-American writer and daughter of two immigrants, is a fairly new writer currently teaching literature and composition courses in her local colleges in the Bay Area. Her most recent publications were in university magazines at CSU East Bay. She is also involved in international programs as well, including summer international exchange leadership programs with other universities, working with international students in year long learning communities, as well as teaching in a language immersion program.

A Phone Call To the Azores

was always fun to watch.
My parents would yell into the phone
saliva spattering from their lips
as they made sure the relatives could hear them.
I could hear my aunt's shrilly voice
across the states and the Atlantic,
see her hand pressing the phone against her face,
her other arm extended, palm open wide,
"Oh my God! How *are* you, my filha?"

Letters took 2 weeks to get anywhere
so Sundays at 2pm, our time, were reserved for the phone.
My mom would say, "Be nice.
In the old days people used to yell across the canyon.
We didn't have telephones on the islands."
We'd all wait our turn to say a quick hello
then pass the phone down the line of people waiting.

When I was 8, over 20 family members sat on Avó's porch.
My uncle played his guitar. The women brought out food.
We all squeezed onto this concrete pad at night
with pillows and blankets keeping us warm.
I could only see glimpses of faces,
arms clasped together, bare feet tapping the floor.
We were singing, eating, laughing
because there were no telephones in 1992.
All we had were those conversations on the porch,
a family of faces we could barely see.

Immigration Tuesday at the Masonic Center

The stone building offered nothing
that I would come to this country for,
but every Tuesday, thousands flow
into the Masonic Center, waiting
to be led to something better.

What's wrong with Portugal, I asked my Dad.
It's just not home anymore.

As we climbed the steps into
this building, solicitors waved voting papers
in our faces. I took one and threw it away.

While waiting for the ceremony to begin,
I stepped outside. I was met by a man selling
placards for everyone's certificates. I bought one,
just so he would leave me alone.
I turned into the building for the last time that day
and waited for the show to begin.

I saw eager eyes ready to promise
themselves to America with little flags waving in the air.
They stood below their families in the balcony and swore
to defend our country, to protect our laws, half of them
not understanding what they just repeated.

After the oath, we walked outside and stood still
on the steps of the building and filled out his voting card.
I had to read most of it to him, but like everyone else,
he wanted to belong here.

On our way back to the ferry building,
everyone was holding their certificates with both hands.
I reached into my bag and gave my Dad his placard
so he could keep his paper safe.

Working For a Better Future

It's quiet in those offices at night.
Only the buzz of fluorescent bulbs pierces that kind of silence
until the plastic wheels of the cart roll out of the janitor's closet.
In the distance, a whisper from a radio,
stale popcorn left on top of the trash.
My dad pushes his cart,
one black bag hanging from his back pocket, smiling
moving with the steady beat of the cart's rhythm.
I can see the gray sprouting from above his ears
that persistent wrinkle trapped
between the crease of his cheek and his tired eyes.

Senta–te aqui e brinca com teu irmão
he'd tell me every time so that we didn't get our hands dirty
pushing the cart.

He always liked the help, but knew we'd forget
a hidden can, a watermark on the desk of someone important,
a piece of gum stuck to the black plastic bags in the trash cans.
He couldn't trust two kids to dust or vacuum.
So we'd sit until sleep rolled over us
like a full trash cart on the carpet
streaking our faces with yawns
and our jackets became litter draping over our bodies.

When I was old enough, he taught me to push the cart,
to know its weight, its size, to feel the pressure
it pushes back when it's full, when he was full
of sleep. He'd push through until 2 a.m.
making sure everyone's trash was disposed of.
He'd turn off the lights, leaving only clean floors
and empty trashcans.
Gostas de ajudar agora borboleta mas a 40 anos ...

The silence in my bedroom at 2 a.m. keeps me awake now.

Everything perfectly still like the desks we'd clean.
The darkness ties its bag around me and closes
leaving me alone with the trash I've created,
the planner stuffed with post–its I can't throw away,
the commute I committed to so that I wouldn't
have the cart to push at night—

Não sei se este carro vai me deixar.

Will I Ever Be Home?

Every other year, I'd sit in the Pico airport,
a tiny, non–air conditioned airport
while my Mom squeezed in every last minute
with the parade of people
hanging off of the back of a pick up truck,
hugging them stronger than
she'd ever hugged me.
I couldn't miss them yet
like my mom did.
We all knew it was temporary.

My grandma used to pack
some bread, butter, and cheese sandwiches
and buy me a Kima.
For the long road ahead, she'd say.
We were always on the road,
back and forth to this country.

Seven years ago,
I left the Azores for good
or so it seemed to my family,
except for Avô. He knew I'd be back.

No one came to wish me goodbye
that time. I tried to say it,
but couldn't. He stood there,
tears welling up in his eyes,
four years of eating alone,
and no one to share his home with

blown into a cloth handkerchief.
His face sagged now with age,
his eyelids drooped and he'd gone
through half a pack of cigarettes
on the road here.

My Portuguese survival kit
of bread and butter ended
when Avô's pain began.
he replaced it with what he could:
a beer and a ham and cheese sandwich
bought at the airport.
He hugged me the way my mom used to
hug her family
and I embraced him,
told him, *Don't cry, Avô,*
It's not goodbye.

Now, I can't even remember
the smell of his cigarettes,
the color of his hair,
the wrinkles on his face.

I should have held on longer.

Fado In a Portuguese Hall In Petaluma, Ca

The doors open to swarms of Holy Ghost members
with *Matanza* tickets in their hands.
The pig is hanging near the music stage,
its rib cage held open with bamboo spears,
its body decorated with red and pink flowers.
The bar begins to fill up with men looking to celebrate
after a day of cutting up pig meat for 300 people.
Widowed sisters from *São Miguel* are selling *filhós*. $5 a bag.
The rumble of voices bounces off the walls
as people file into their reserved bench seating
and women with bandanas start delivering free wine,
Carlo Rossi Merlot in plastic cups. For everyone.
Juices cost 2 tickets. Tickets cost $1.
Tables begin to rise, one by one,
to choose from the buffet of pork meat,
yams, and an American potato salad.
After dinner, the folklore dancing begins.
Women in short layered skirts, aprons, and braids
begin circling men in short pants and ruffled white shirts.
Everyone claps, whistles.
A 20 year old recorded cassette crackles while they dance.
As they exit, a singer enters on stage.
She's 40ish, accent like mine.
Everyone sits, eyes glued to her
as if she was a prophet.
She sings of home, of farming, of love and longing.
I see an old woman close her eyes
puts her hand over her heart
when the singer's voice pierces the silence.
Does she see the ocean, feel the salt spray?

Provar: To Taste

Prova isto. É bom. My Grandpa always wanted us to try new things even if we didn't know if we were going to like them. He hands me a single grape that no longer smells like a grape. It is a purple globe, but it is so full of liquid, the skin is about to burst. I watch as he lifts his face to the sun, his straw hat stuck to his forehead by dried up sweat. He places two grapes in his mouth and then another. The popping sound they made was like… His eyes squint and his lips pull back to show his teeth as if he was in pain. I let the grape roll around in my palm for a few seconds and then pick it up with two fingers, gently. I tilt my head back just like my Avô did, lift my hand into the air. My mom sees my hand in the air, laughs, and pushes it away, "She can't eat those! Oh *Pai*, she's not like me. She wasn't raised here."

I stood there, mouth open, eyes closed until I heard my mom laugh again. My grandpa always tells me I am Portuguese so why wasn't I allowed to try this? For many years my mom protected me from anything that wasn't American. The visits to Pico started the year of my first birthday and this summer I was eight years old. By the time my mom was eight she was allowed to have a glass of homemade wine right from the barrel.

The next day, I want to try again. Mom and Grandma are upstairs cooking. I wander downstairs to the wine cellar where Avô is filling his white plastic wine jugs. His friend stood there, his green jeans torn at the knees, his shoes scuffed and covered in fine brown dirt. His plaid shirt is soaking in sweat and faded from the sun. He asks my grandpa if I was the "American granddaughter."

Avô straightened out his back after emptying the clear hose of wine and answered, "Yes, but when she's here, *Ela é portuguesa.*"

I could still hear my mom talking upstairs through the thin flooring above us. She couldn't hear me. Avô reaches into a clear glass wine jug filled with a light purple juice and at the bottom, over 20 puffed out grapes bob a little when he picks it up. It had been tucked behind a giant wine barrel so my grandma couldn't find it. It looks filthy and even has a cobweb glued between the handle and the opening. How could he drink that, let alone take a sip out of something so dirty? He gives the jug a good swirl and scoops out a grape. Again he says, *Prova.*

The man standing there with us smiled, the side of his mouth lifts slightly more than the other. I take the grape. This time I bite right into it, waiting for the sweet taste of September harvest. My entire face begins to pucker and my tongue locks in place, frozen with liquid fire burning it. He tells me to swallow the liquid, then chew on the flesh of the grape.

I could hear him say, "Maybe she is American."

The other man laughs like my mom had earlier so I did as I was told and the burning stopped. I feel warm inside, a kind of heat that a tropical sun couldn't mimic. There is a curious tingling in my chest I did not recognize, but I am learning to enjoy today. I ask for another.

Toma quidad. São doce mas picao, Avô says to me as he hands me another.

Their faces are contorted in laughter that looked like the grin of a horse as its lips pull back and its big square teeth open to receive a treat. Avô bends down to cork the wine jugs and sends the man on his way. He tilts his hat, smiles, and reminds me that I still have to make it back up the stairs. Avô gives me the glass jug and lets me try to swirl it around. It is the size of two milk gallons combined. I hug it, clasping my fingertips on the other side. My whole body swirls with it and a few drops splash up out of the top onto my face. It smells like the sweet wine Avô makes, like a strong grape juice. I let the jug slide down my legs to the floor and wipe the liquid off my face with my index finger. It is thicker than water, almost clear like it too with only one drop on my finger. I taste it. It is bitter, not sweet like the grape. It is hot, like rubbing alcohol is hot on an open wound, then cool as I take a deep breath.

He motions me to go upstairs and tucks the jug behind the barrels, then picks me up, places me on his shoulders and carries me up the steps.

A Confiançar: To Trust

"All right, tell your brother I need his friend to look at my mom's car. Her brakes need to be redone. We can trust him right?" I ask my husband.

Ben looks at me, bites his lip, "I think so."

Sunday arrives way too fast. My mom decides to make this a whole day event. Everyone's invited to our Sunday dinner after the car is fixed. My brother–in–law and his friend pull up in a truck I could almost walk under, blaring country music. His friend jumps down and introduces himself to my dad first, "Hey there! I'm CJ. I hear there's a problem with your brakes?"

He is wearing old jeans with whitened spots where his knees are, a t–shirt with a woman in a bikini holding a Budweiser. He's clean–shaven, but his hat covers the top of his face. He kneels down, one hand on the car, the other on the concrete.

"Well Josh, let's get her up in the air. Gotta take the tires off to check her out."

My parents have moved back and are now standing by the garage door, arms folded like two… watching these two men they have to trust to help them.

"*Não sei se eu gosta de isto. São puro americanos,*" my mom says to my dad, shaking her head. Her right foot is now tapping the ground.

"*Vamos a ver.* Can you fix it?" my dad says to her, watching CJ as a child watches his parent to learn something new. "CJ, right? You like to have a drink? I can bring something."

CJ smiles and laughs, "I don't know, sure. What do ya got?"

I follow my dad into the garage. We pull out a jug of old moonshine from behind the curtain. It's covered in dust from the wind and rain that sneaks in when we open the garage door year after year. My dad doesn't wipe it off, just unscrews the cap and pours it into six liqueur glasses, never spilling a drop from the large mouth of the jug into the tiny glasses. He preserves every drop, but fills each glass to the top.

"Let's see if he can handle it, that tough guy," he says to me and laughs almost under his breath, then takes a quick shot of moonshine from the jug. We each take three glasses out, balancing them between our ten fingers. He doesn't ask anyone else if they want some, just hands them each a glass. "Here, try," he says to Josh and CJ.

"I do enjoy a good drink," CJ says to my dad. "Mmm smells sweet, like juice. What is it?"

"Moonshine," my dad instructs him.

"Oh yeah. My grandpa used to make this stuff. Used to drink it with him all the time."

CJ watches my parents and me clink glasses and drink in one gulp. One collective, refreshing "Ahhh" and nothing left in the glasses but the smell of blackberries. Ben stands next to me, defending his small sips. My mom lets him know he's ok. "At least he likes it." Ben tries to warn them that it has a little kick, something that takes time to learn to appreciate.

CJ and Josh look at each other and smirk. They hold the glass with two greasy fingers, fanning out their pinkies. They eat the berry with the other hand and seem to enjoy it, then drink the syrupy liquid. One shot, two men hunched over gasping for air. "Wow! Holy crap! Who made this?" CJ tries to hold his composure.

"We did. In the kitchen," my dad says to him, almost innocently.

We all start laughing at the American boys who can't keep up with my 5–foot mom and gringo husband.

"Don't worry about it boys, most Americans can't handle it," I tell them grinning, my teeth pushing through my lips.

EDUARDO BETTENCOURT PINTO

Eduardo Bettencourt Pinto was born in Gabela, Angola in 1954 and has lived in Canada since 1983. He has published several books of poetry and fiction. His most recent book of bilingual poetry is *Travelling with Shadows* (English and Portuguese). In Portuguese: *A Cor do Sul nos teus Olhos*, poetry (2012), and *Aubrianne* (2013) fiction, in a chapbook format. He is represented in several anthologies and collective books in Portugal, Angola, Brazil, England, United States, Canada, Latvia and Cuba.

A mãe da minha vida

> Só há um modo de escapar de um lugar:
> é sairmos de nós. Só há um modo de sairmos de nós:
> é amarmos alguém.
> – Mia Couto, *A confissão da leoa*

A bengala repousa à sua esquerda. Está sentada na varanda. Os seus pensamentos escorrem como o murmúrio da água da fonte, uma escultural deusa de silêncio e cimento de cujas mãos parece brotar um regato inominável.

Pisca os olhos de vez em quando, modorrentos. Não sei se pela cadência monótona da água ou pelo bafo quente da tarde. O certo é que o seu olhar está poisado no vazio, num deserto.

Os idosos têm uma maneira estranha de comunicar com os anjos. Fazem–no através dos seus mortos. Os mais otimistas, porém, recorrem à memória como forma de diálogo com o passado. A morte é mais do que uma ausência e do que um mergulho na terra. É o paradigma da efemeridade.

A minha mãe faz hoje noventa anos. Sinto–a ausente, distante. Sento–me ao seu lado e abraço–a.

Pois é … – diz.

Não digo nada. O silêncio de alguns momentos deve ser preservado. É como se estivéssemos num templo a ouvir o cântico de pedras sagradas.

Não sei como chegou a esta idade.

«As pessoas esquecem até que estão vivas», disse Mia Couto. É verdade. Distraí–me estes anos todos. Andei por desertos, savanas, rios, oceanos, montanhas, vilas e cidades. Observei uma guerra por dentro: o tombar das sua vítimas, os seus heróis e algozes de pólvora e retórica. Descobri em muitos homens o desapiedado olhar do Diabo. Noutros, a transparente ressonância dos anjos. Tive filhos. (Desde então, confesso, há um fantasma a correr atrás de mim). Escrevi livros, plantei árvores. Alimentei pássaros e cães. Esgravatei a terra à procura do Sol. Encontrei, no topo das montanhas, a sabedoria e o silêncio de Deus. Nas mulheres, a tragédia e a exaltação, o delírio, poesia, a música das árvores, o ressoo mais inaudível das flores. Vivi, meu Deus!, se vivi. Mas no espelho dos meus dias, naquele momento único em que estou comigo mesmo, com a minha essência de homem, acabo sempre por descobrir na imagem dentro de mim o menino a correr pela rua da ausência e dos mitos.

Há momentos em que a sinto em África. Nero ladrava no quintal, corria desenfreadamente e atirava–se ao portão com a fúria de um tigre. Uma silhueta dava um pulo no passeio. Ouvia–se uma imprecação. Ela ria–se, os cotovelos apoiados no muro da varanda.

Eram momentos felizes.

Vejo, através da neblina dos anos, a mão de minha mãe a guiar–me pelas ruas da sua ilha.

Nasci do seu ventre, dos seus braços, das suas mãos e do seu colo. Nasci das suas lágrimas e do seu riso. E foi na sua voz que ouvi o mar pela primeira vez.

Na minha infância, que passou por mim com o delírio e a cintilação fulminante de uma miríade de imagens, a minha mãe era a minha casa.

Estávamos em África.

O meu pai era a árvore onde pousavam as mais esquivas aves daqueles dias. Por vezes era um trovão a cair do teto da casa, assustador e feroz. As paredes tremiam e eu sentia um aperto na bexiga. Apetecia–me fugir para muito longe, esconder–me atrás do sol ou da lua ou no último andar de um prédio. As árvores do quintal ofereciam troncos esguios; os arbustos eram coisas hirsutas e vulneráveis onde só os insetos se podiam ocultar.

Tudo passou: África, o meu pai, a idade dos frutos. Os meus irmãos são agora vozes longínquas no outro lado da linha telefónica. Fiquei órfão de um tempo que já morreu.

Aqui estamos os dois, minha mãe e eu, juntos como duas palmeiras plantadas na beira da estrada. Fustigou–nos o vento, as chuvas, o frio, a neve das lágrimas e da nostalgia. A sua frondosa sombra, porém, protege–me da ardência solar nos dias mais ardentes do destino; e nas noites longas e luminosas é a memória que deixa sobre mim cintilações da lua e o silêncio peregrino do passado.

Os seus olhos, cansados e perscrutadores, aproximam–se dos meus. São o mar de Setembro: doces, serenos, terrivelmente belos de tanto amor.

–Pois é ... –diz, apertando entre as mãos a doce luz da tarde.

The Mother of My Life (Trans.)

> There is only one way to escape from a place:
> to leave oneself. There is only one way to leave oneself:
> to love someone.
>   –Mia Couto, *A confissão da leoa (Confession of a Lioness)*

The cane rests on her left side. She's on the porch, seated. Her thoughts run like the murmur of a water fountain, a sculptural goddess of silence and cement from whose hands seem to sprout a nameless stream.

Drowsy, she blinks her eyes once in a while. I don't know if it is due to the monotonous cadence of the water or by the hot afternoon breath. The truth is, her glance rests in emptiness, on a desert.

The elderly have a strange way of communicating with angels. They accomplish this through their dead. The most optimistic, however, resort to memory as a form of dialoguing with the past. Death is more than an absence and a plunge to the ground. It's the paradigm of the ephemeral.

My mother is ninety today. I feel her absent, distant. I sit next to her and hug her.

– Yeah...–She says.

I say nothing. The silence of some moments should be preserved. It's like we are in a temple hearing the singing of sacred stones.

I don't know how she got to her age.

"People forget they are even alive," says Mia Couto. It's true. I was distracted all these years. I walked through deserts, savannas, rivers, oceans, mountains, villages and cities. I watched a war from within: the tumble of its victims, heroes and tyrants of gunpowder and rhetoric. I discovered in many men the heartless eye of the devil and, in others, the transparent resonance of angels. I had children. (Since then, I confess, there is a ghost running after me). I wrote books and planted trees. I fed birds and dogs. I scraped the earth in search of the sun. I found the wisdom and the silence of God at the top of the mountains. In women, tragedy and exhilaration, delirium, poetry, the music of trees, the most inaudible resound of flowers. I lived, my God, if I lived! However, in the mirror of my days, in that unique moment in which I am with myself, with my essence as a man, I always end up discovering the image of the boy within me running across the street of absence and myths.

There are times when I feel her back in Africa. Barking in the yard and running, Nero throwing himself against the gate, wildly, with the fury of a tiger. A silhouette would jump on the sidewalk and I could hear a curse. She would laugh, her elbows resting on the wall of the porch.

They were happy times.

I see, through the mist of years, my mother's hand leading me in the streets of her island.

I was born from her womb, her arms, hands, and her lap. I was born from her tears and her laughter. And it was in her voice that I heard the sea for the first time.

In my childhood, that passed by me with delirium and a fulminant flicker of myriad images, my mother was my home.

We were in Africa.

My father was the tree where the most elusive birds of those days landed. Sometimes he was a thunder, falling from the ceiling, scary and fierce. The walls shook, and I felt a tightness in my bladder. I felt like running very far away and hiding behind the Sun or the Moon or on the top floor of a building. The trees in the yard offered slender trunks; plants were hirsute and vulnerable places for the insects to hide.

Everything has passed: Africa, my father, the age of the fruits. My brothers are now distant voices on the other side of the telephone line. I became an orphan of a time that has died.

Here we are, the two of us, my mother and I, together as two palm trees planted on the roadside. The wind whipped us, the rain, the cold, the snow of tears and nostalgia. Its leafy shade, however, protects me from the blazing sun in the warmest days of destiny; in the long and bright nights, she is the memory that leaves over me a flickering moon and the pilgrim silence of the past.

Her eyes, tired and probing, are near mine. They are the September sea: sweet, serene, terribly beautiful with so much love.

– Yeah...–She says, pressing between her hands the sweet afternoon light.

Angola

A voz treme, arde dentro do grito: inocência da rosa.
Palavras, ínfimos desertos, alucinações: o poema.
Inútil ave na fome das crianças, perdida semente
entre a madrugada e o desespero dos que tombam
sob os muros da guerra.
Um voltear de cinzas: dançam nas lágrimas os fantasmas
das ideologias. Resta–nos, agarrados aos escombros
dos mitos, a esperança; petrificada, orvalhada de sombras,
reflectida nos espelhos de outras estações.
Resta–nos o poema, caído entre os cactos do desespero,
perdido no deserto do silêncio.

Angola (Trans.)

The voice trembles, burns within a cry: innocence of the rose.
Words, tiny deserts, hallucinations: the poem.
Useless bird in children's hunger, lost seed
between the dawn and the despair of those who fall
under the walls of the war.
A flicker of ashes: on those tears dance the ghosts
of ideologies.
For us remains, clinging to debris
of myths, hope; petrified, dewy shadows,
reflected in the mirrors of other seasons.
We just have the poem, fallen among cactus of despair
lost in the desert of silence.

A poesia

Ficam algumas sílabas, poucas.
Quero dizer: a acesa vela da insónia,
a roupa abandonada no pó
da cadeira,
a janela aberta às sombras
das magnólias.
A lenta respiração
do mundo.

Poetry (Trans.)

A few syllables remain.
I mean: a lit candle of insomnia,
clothes abandoned in the dust's
chair,
the window opened to the magnolia's
shadows.
The slow breathing
of the world.

Mulher a jardinar

Quando toca numa flor,
as suas mãos tornam–se
nas pétalas da primavera.

Woman Gardening (Trans.)

When she touches a flower,
her hands become
the petals of spring.

BRIAN SOUSA

Rhode Island native Brian Sousa has been published in various journals including *Verdad, Newfound, Quiddity, Redivider, Gavea–Brown, The Writer, Babilonia,* the *DMQ Review* and others; he also has poetry and fiction forthcoming in the *Atticus Review* and the *St. Petersburg Review.* His fiction is also featured in the Rutgers University Press anthology of Luso–American Literature, 2011. In 2007, he was awarded a fellowship by the Rhode Island State Council on the Arts, and in 2011, he was a finalist for the Dzanc Books International Literary Award, and winner of a scholarship to the Dzanc Books International Literary Program in Portugal. His first book, *Almost Gone* (Tagus / UPNE Press) was published in March 2013. Sousa holds an MFA from Emerson College, is an editor for the music and culture website *Mule Variations*, and plays guitar in the indie–rock band Ocean*Transfer.

Just One Night
(Nuno, 1975)

Nuno squeezed the letter so tightly that his hand shook. A loose wave of dizziness hit him, and he leaned against the wall. All around him, Helena's old dresses hung silently, like old ghosts.

He'd been digging through cardboard boxes, looking for that picture, the drawing that Helena had done of him playing football long ago. Paulo was trying out for the team next week, and Nuno was going to tack it up in his room, surprise him with it.

But the letter had found him first, folded neatly and tucked inside of a small wooden jewelry box. That was the thing too; it wasn't crumpled up, but put away carefully. The letter was from Mateo. After all of these years, it was really written in the way that Nuno had imagined he would write it—like a damn woman. There were hearts drawn on the side of the page, and even the faded letters were curly.

Nuno closed his eyes and everything came back. The sight of Mateo's pale face on the bed, the sand all over the blankets. How Nuno had crept away alone, leaving Helena there. She hadn't seen him, he was sure of that. And he'd never told her that he was there that night. He'd tried, in the days that followed, but he hadn't been able to. And slowly, the days and months and years piled over it, bringing a home thousands of miles away, and children, and new worries and problems. But that awful guilt had followed him everywhere, hadn't it? There was no escaping it. Nuno tried to breathe deeply, tried to calm himself down, but it was no use. He slumped against the wall and waited for the nausea to pass. Thank God Helena wasn't home.

He knew he wasn't innocent. Sure, it scared him. But he'd lived a long life already. He'd done good things and bad. He still believed in God, but he wasn't really sure what happened when people died. What would happen to him? But what was done was done. There was no going back, that was for sure.

Finally, Nuno opened his eyes and pushed his feet forward. How long had he been standing in this goddamn closet? It was dumb, really, all of it. There was nothing he could do. The past was the past. Helena would be home from Mass soon. There was still half the lawn to mow, and he'd left a cold beer on the counter. He put everything back in the box the way it was, shoved it into the shadows, and closed the door.

But as he walked downstairs, everything felt sucked of color. The sunlight poured through the windows, but it was ugly, heavy, and hot. Nuno swigged his beer, but it was warm. He poured it down the sink, watching the foam disappear. For the first time in thirty–four years, he felt different. About everything. He wasn't what had changed. But something was off.

When Helena pulled into the driveway, Nuno was sitting at the kitchen table, his usual spot. The door slammed, and he heard her talking to herself. He worried more about her driving alone lately. Her knees and ankles were tight with arthritis, and she didn't pay enough attention to the road. She was stubborn, though. She still insisted on driving to the few places that she went to frequently—church, the doctor's office, the supermarket, Paulo's school—and she wouldn't take no for an answer. Sometimes Nuno wondered if the medication had changed her. If she could change back.

He'd been paging through a soccer magazine that he'd bought for Paulo, unable to focus.

He'd ask her about the letter right away. Why she'd kept it. What she knew. What she had been keeping from him all these years.

But when she finally walked in, bringing with her a burst of humid August air, Nuno couldn't say anything. He just listened as she groaned.

"It's too hot," she panted, dropping a sagging brown bag of groceries on the table before him. "Chicken for dinner." Nuno peered at her intently. Her forehead was damp with sweat, and some strands of graying hair were pasted to her face. She used to be beautiful, he thought. She was still pretty, though. Older–looking, but pretty. Was he still handsome? He knew that, could feel that his entire body had begun to shrink and droop with age over the last few years.

"I thought you were going to church?"

Helena checked the clock on the stove and then walked to the windowsill, where she kept her pills. He'd been surprised that there were so many, but they seemed to be working. After coming home that day and finding her all wrapped up in that business with the dog, Nuno just wanted her to get better. The doctor had made them go see another doctor together, a psychiatrist, and she called what had happened to Helena an "episode," prescribed a bunch of medication, and said that it would "take years to get to the heart of what caused it." The psychiatrist's office smelled like tobacco, and there were strange posters on the walls, of planets and pyramids. When they left, Nuno told Helena that they could handle their problems at home, together, without the woman who glared at him as if *he'd* done something wrong. What had he done? He'd convinced Mr. Costa not to go to the police and forgiven his wife for what she did. That was more than enough. He didn't need to sit in some woman's office and tell her how he felt about the whole goddamn thing.

Helena swallowed, sighed, and sat across from him. "I did. Short Mass. And then I go to pick up grocery."

Her English had improved, but she still screwed up a lot. Nuno didn't think she really cared about learning the language. Some days, he would correct her, but today he could only watch her silently. She picked up the soccer magazine, shrugged, and tossed it down. Then she smiled tiredly.

"What's the matter? You don't look good. You need to eat?" She kneaded her face with her hands. "I'll start soon, don't worry."

Nuno shook his head, finished his beer. "Where's Paulo?"

"He's running on the beach, Nuno, like you told him to."

"I don't think so."
Helena opened the refrigerator and peered inside.

"He should be running every day. He's not going to make it." Nuno waited as Helena nodded absently and moved her lips, talking to herself as she planned dinner. When she didn't respond, he left the room, wondering how much she really listened to him.

Paulo was quiet at the table, pushing bread into his mouth. His eyes were red.

"What were you doing at the beach?" Nuno asked.

"Running. Swimming."

"By yourself?"

"Yup."

"When do tryouts start?"

"You already asked me that, Dad," he said, his mouth full. His hair and his shirt were still wet.

"So?"

"Tomorrow."

"Well, what time?"

Paulo shrugged, signaling Helena to pass the butter dish. He mashed some onto his bread with a knife.

"Paulo, I need to know so I can bring you. There might be traffic."

"There's no traffic on Saturdays," he mumbled.

"Well, we should get there early, anyway."

"I don't want you to stay and watch," he said quickly, "and Chris can give me a ride home."

"Who's Chris?" asked Helena.

"He's trying out too. He's—"

"Not an athlete," Nuno snapped. Helena stared at him. He thought of her staring at Mateo, resting her head on his chest. "I will always remember the first night," the letter had read. What had happened the first night? Nuno's stomach churned.

"Why don't you want me to watch?" he asked, trying to keep his voice calm. "My father always watched me, in Portugal, you know? He told me what to do to get better, he helped—"

"No, I don't want you to," said Paulo. He looked to Helena, but she pushed her food across her plate with her fork.

"Fine," Nuno said, "fine."

Paulo stared at him for a second. "Can I go?" he said.

"Where?" Helena asked.

"To watch TV," he said, standing and dumping his empty plate on the counter.

"Paulo, I made cookies," she called. "Paulo!"

Nuno and Helena sat there in the new emptiness, staring at each other. Nuno had always loved her eyes. They had faded, and the right eye was now the pale blue of the sky, while the left was a dull green. Nuno thought they were even more beautiful the way they were now.

Right then, Nuno wanted to tell her that he knew. That he'd always known. That he'd been there that night. That he'd watched her kneel down and begin to sob. "How could you?" she would whisper, and then her heavy steps would echo as she ran upstairs and slammed the door.

But Helena just sat there, drumming her fingers softly on the table. Nuno had noticed that since she'd been taking the medicine regularly, she'd been much more fidgety. She'd also started smoking more.

"Cigarette," she said as she walked toward the front door. "I clean after." That night Nuno stayed downstairs and watched TV long after Paulo, and then Helena, went to bed. When Helena said goodnight to Paulo, she kissed his cheek and she rubbed his back.

"Sleep well," she said in the way that she always did, starting low and ending on a high note. "'Night, Dad," Paulo said as he went upstairs.

"Goodnight!" Nuno yelled loudly, and Helena looked over, scowling.

"I'm going up," she said. "Are you okay? You feel sick?"

He shook his head and watched as she slowly maneuvered out of the room. The blue lines of her veins climbed her calves.

Nuno could barely watch TV. Were they always this quiet around him? Something still felt off, and he couldn't put his finger on it. A beer might help, but he was tired and didn't feel like it.

It was warm out, and he walked out the front door and stood on the doorstep. It had been a good summer for the garden. Nuno had dug it out a bit and made it longer and wider this year, added some soil. In the shine of the moon he could see the cherry tomato plants weighed down with fruit. He inhaled the salt in the air and remembered Lagos. How different everything was. How, days after everything happened, Helena had come right up to him and touched her finger to his lower lip, where she'd cut him.

"I'm sorry," she had said.

"I'm sorry, too," he'd said. And that was that. Well, in some ways. She hadn't said one word about it since then, either. Not one word.

Nuno shut the door and climbed the stairs. It was a mistake. That's what Antonio called it in the days afterward, before he and Nuno stopped talking to each other altogether. A mistake.

The door to the bedroom was cracked open, but the room seemed darker than usual.

Nuno searched for the light on the night table, knocking a book to the floor. Helena coughed and her eyes switched on.

When Nuno slid into bed, sleep wouldn't come. His finger lingered on his bottom lip. It had faded into a tiny mark, like a dimple. He remembered the way Helena swung her arm, the sudden taste of blood. His head spun and he rolled it across the pillow. His eyes clung to the crescent on the floor, the light from the hallway. It felt as though his life had become someone else's, but Nuno knew that wasn't true, it wasn't true at all. This life had always been his. He'd just chosen to ignore it.

Helena pressed against him, facing away. Nuno wanted, suddenly, to hold onto her as tightly as he could to stop the feeling that was washing over him, as if he was adrift in those waves again, being tossed by the current. It was out of his control, all of it. His heart drummed under the covers, and he yanked the covers down.

He rubbed his hands up and down Helena's legs. Eventually, she pulled him toward her.

Her breath came long and easy now and her movements were slow, mechanical. Was she bored? Did she not want him anymore? Nuno tensed suddenly, and she reached back, feeling with her hand.

In the dim light, Nuno saw Mateo's face appear—the straight white gleam of his smile, the long locks of hair—and he knew that Helena had done this with him. That maybe she'd loved Mateo more than she could love him.

"What's the matter?" Helena whispered hesitantly.
Nuno rolled onto his back. His upper lip was wet.

"It's all right, dear," Helena said, rolling over. "It's all right. You must be getting sick." She was asleep within minutes.

Nuno awoke slowly and brought his knees up to his chest, waiting for his legs to brush Helena's. But they never did. He opened his eyes. The clock said nine.

"Where were you?" asked Paulo, glancing up from the table. Helena placed a mug of steaming coffee in front of Nuno as he sat down.

"There are more pancakes," she said over her shoulder. "We were waiting."

Paulo gulped his juice. "Are you sick? It's so late."

"Why didn't you wake me?" Nuno asked Helena groggily.

"Maybe you needed it," she said, coming over and putting a hand on his shoulder. "Your body needed it. You feel better?"

Nuno could smell the grease on her oven mitt. "Sure," he said. Paulo stood up. The shirt he was wearing said "The Beatles" in faded lettering. "Where did you get that?"

"What?"

"That shirt."

"I've had this for a year. What time are we leaving?"

Nuno stared at him. Tryouts. "We're leaving at ten."

"That's in a half hour!"

"Right. Get ready."

Paulo dragged his way upstairs.

"Did he say something?"

"I didn't hear anything." Helena piled pancakes on his plate and filled his coffee cup to the brim, so that it would be impossible to lift without spilling.

"Nuno, it happen to everyone. Never happen before, right? Maybe just one time, that's it. *Não se preocupe.*"

Nuno sat there and stared ahead, past the bottles of pills on the windowsill, out to where the sun was shining. Helena was cleaning up, whistling to herself. She paused and followed his gaze.

"Better get those tomatoes soon," she warned. "Ripe. Ready to burst."

There was no traffic as they drove to the field.

"We're going to be there so early," said Paulo, rolling down his window. "Can you open your window?"

"You want to be there early," Nuno said, cranking it down, "so the coach knows you care. Trust me, now. Is it still Coach—"

"Davis? Yeah."

"Ah, you need a Portuguese coach. Davis doesn't know what he's doing."

"He's fine."

"You nervous?"

Paulo didn't say anything, just looked out the window. Nuno saw he had his fist clenched in his lap.

"It's okay to be nervous, Paulo. I used to get—"

"I'm fine, Dad," he said, as they pulled down the dirt road to the soccer fields.

"Thanks," he said, jumping out.

Nuno watched the other boys on the field. No one really looked at Paulo. They were all standing around, talking, laughing with one another. A few of them were kicking the ball around. Nuno wished someone would call out to his son. He had a friend or two here, right?

"Okay," said Paulo, putting his bag over his shoulder and backing away.

"Well, maybe I'll stay for a bit," Nuno said.

"There's no other parents here," Paulo said over his shoulder as he walked away, "and Mom promised you wouldn't. Please don't, all right? Please?"

Nuno put the car in drive and pulled away.

It was almost eleven. There wouldn't be a game on at the Lusitania Club until at least one, and that was if he was lucky.

It was dark in the club and the TV was bright. Soccer highlights were on— Portugal in the 1966 World Cup semifinal against England nine years ago. They'd lost. Nuno took his favorite stool, and Luis walked over, holding the newspaper.

"Early!" he said. "Sporting isn't on 'til one today."

Nuno shrugged and forced a grin. "How about red?"

He drank gratefully, gazing at the television. Luis walked over and leaned against the bar.
"How's Paulo?"
"At tryouts."

"And Helena?"

"Doing good. How's Kim?"

Luis cleared his throat. "She's okay."

Nuno nodded. His wine was nearly gone. Luis was staring at him blankly. Nuno glanced away from him. The night that it had happened, he'd gone to the club to watch Sporting in the UEFA Cup. Luis hadn't been there, and everyone was drunk, including Kim, who was bartending. After she closed, she led him out to the parking lot, where they started kissing, huddled together in the darkness.

"Let's go somewhere," he'd said. They'd ended up at a crappy hotel on a bed with stained sheets, both sneaking home after a few hours to lie about where they'd been.

He noticed how tired Luis looked. "The thing is, Nuno," he said, "Kim ain't doing so well."

Suddenly Nuno remembered the way Kim's hair smelled like dark rum that night, the way it fell across his face.

"What's wrong?"

Luis stared at the clock above the bar and sighed. "She got cancer."

"Shit. I'm sorry."

Nuno's face felt itchy and hot. Once he'd realized, after it happened, that Kim wasn't going to tell Luis, he'd been able to relax a little. He still felt terrible. But it was only that one time, and he was drunk. Kim got a job at another bar, and he never saw her anymore. Things happened. He couldn't go back and fix it.

"More wine?"

Nuno nodded. The phone rang in the back room, and Luis put the bottle down next to his glass and walked away.

That night Nuno lay in bed, motionless. During the game, a bunch of guys had come in and they'd stayed out afterward, drinking wine, bullshitting. Dinner had passed by blurrily. Paulo had said he was tired from tryouts and gone to bed early, and there was nothing on TV.

Helena spat into the sink in the bathroom and hummed to herself. Nuno wondered if she was upset about the night before. Maybe she was right, it was a one–time thing. It happened to everyone. She'd acted normal at dinner, but a few times he'd caught her looking at him oddly.

The important thing was to stop thinking about it. But the thought of trying again didn't excite him like it usually did. It actually made him nervous.

Nuno put his magazine down as she turned off the light on her side. They lay there, not touching. Was she waiting for him, or was she hoping that he didn't try anything? For a second, Nuno wanted to just walk away. There were three beers left in the fridge. He could sit at the table and wait until she fell asleep, and then tell her he'd been sick.

But then he felt Helena's breath on his shoulder.

"Sorry," he said, "I'm not—"

"Shhhh," she whispered, "stop. Let me help you."

In a few seconds her mouth was on him. As he reached down to pull her up, because he knew it was no use, Kim flashed into Nuno's mind. She was bending over the bed, her face turned away.

It felt good. Helena hadn't done this in years. He didn't deserve it. He thought of Mateo, wondered with a hazy start if she'd done this to him, but suddenly it didn't matter. His hand sank into the back of her hair. The darkness was soft and warm and smooth.

"I love you," Nuno said quietly, when they were finished.

But Helena didn't hear him. She was already asleep.

***

Four days later, Nuno was at the club when he decided that it was time to confront Helena. It wasn't just that he kept imagining her with Mateo, it was the idea that she could go on forever not knowing that he *knew*.

"How's Kim?" he asked Luis as he stood up to leave.

Luis shook his head and held up his hand.

Walking into the house, Nuno felt a little unsteady. He wondered where Paulo was. He didn't like him hanging out with Chris; the kid's parents were hippies and Chris had long hair, wore sunglasses, and was a horrible soccer player. Nuno had seen him tripping all over the place at tryouts last year.

He wasn't sure why he'd gotten drunk again. Maybe it was being around Luis lately, the way he avoided Nuno's eyes as he filled his glass. He didn't look as though he'd been sleeping, and he drifted around the bar in a haze.

When Helena walked in, Nuno was staring out the window and watching the rain. She glared at him, dropped the bag on the counter, then peered back outside.

"C'mon, honey," she said loudly. "Don't get wet. Get inside." She whispered something softly in Portuguese that Nuno couldn't make out.

"I'm coming," Paulo said, walking sheepishly. He was soaked, holding his socks and shin guards up against his chest. Helena felt how wet his back was and grimaced. "Go shower, you'll get sick," she ordered.

Paulo nodded and ventured a look at Nuno.
"Well? What happened?"

Helena noisily unloaded the bag of groceries onto the table.

"Did you find out?" Nuno asked, standing and extending his arms.

"Yeah," Paulo said. "I didn't make it."

"Shit!" Nuno slammed his hand on the table. "That fucking guy doesn't know what he's talking about! Coach Davis—"

"It's okay, Dad," called Paulo, escaping upstairs. "It's cool."

"No it's not!" Nuno's voice was louder than he wanted. "It's not okay! That's the problem with you! It's not okay! If you even cared about it, you'd know—"

"It's okay, Nuno," said Helena, stepping in front of him. Her jaw was set and her nostrils flared.

The bathroom door slammed and the shower squeaked on.

"It's okay," she said, nodding, her hands on her hips. "There's next year, right? *Vai dar tudo certo.*"

Nuno crossed his arms and glared at her. This was it. He'd tell her *that he knew* about Mateo. *That he knew* that she'd never truly loved him.

"Helena, listen."

She looked back at him defiantly, her eyebrows raised. Now was the time.

But he couldn't.

"*Certo,*" Nuno said finally, quietly, and sat back down.

The fire in Helena's eyes dimmed. She nodded and walked over to the stove.

Nuno knew at that moment that everything would keep going exactly as it had been in the past. He could almost see the way his life would play out, the way all of their lives would.

And he knew that he would never tell Helena what he'd done.

It was simple. She just didn't need to know.

IAN E. WATTS

Ian E. Watts has roots among the Portuguese of California and Hawai'i. He received his B.A. in Anthropology from the University of Virginia and did graduate work in Portuguese and Brazilian Studies at Brown University. He held grants from the Fundação Oriente, the Instituto Camões and the Fundação Luso-Americana para o Desenvolvimento, and was a research fellow at the National Library of Lisbon. His academic publications include "Bi-racial identity, bi-racial status: Two Chinese orphans raised by the Canossian sisters in Macao," Review of Culture (June 1997) and "Mediating cultural identities: Three Macanese women in the transition" in Macau and its Neighbors toward the 21st century: Proceedings of the International Symposium Organized by the Faculty of Social Sciences and Humanities at the University of Macau, 2-3 June 1997 (University of Macau, 1998). His ethnographic work was adapted to one act of the play Macau 1, 2, 3. More recently, his translations and fiction have appeared in The Brasilia Review and Yellow Chair Review. He resides in New Jersey with his wife and three sons.

praça do comércio

Lisbon's nickname is "The White City." Today it isn't; marble window sashes, door lintels and serpentine sidewalk cobbles are covered in dismal gray. The moonlit lustrous beauty of yesterday's evening shower is no longer; all remaining is late summer's dry heat and dust. Still, Lisbon enchants with its downtown buildings in soft pastels and throngs of beautiful, captivating people. Their eyes, mouths and movements betray practiced languor as they sit in sedate repose smoking cigarettes and drinking coffee; they pay no attention to me as I bolt to the ferry docks.

I stayed on the bus too long and missed too many stops. I asked the Library clerks how I could get to the ferry docks: *cais de balsa*. I guess they only heard docks: *cais*. Or maybe I listened wrong, which is entirely possible. I got off at Cais do Sodré – end of the line for the Cascais–Estoril marginal train – a good fifteen minute sprint to docks near the Praça do Comércio.

Dodging cars, buses and whizzing motorbikes; I practically kill myself getting across avenue after avenue and from square to square. I pass Chinese peddlers hawking shirts wrapped in clear cellophane beside bright green and red plastic animals. A Gypsy shouts out the prices of sunglasses. A scruffy guy bumps into me and opens a well–worn grocery bag:

"It's a good price."

A Nikon.

"No. No thanks," I say and rush on.

I'm close. My landmarks are: a bronze Dom José the–whatever on horseback trampling serpents; a triumphal arch with Glory crowning Ingenuity and Valor–it has the inscription: *virtutibus maiorum ut sit omnibus documento*, p.p.d. The greatest of virtues teaches all. What? I wish I kept up with my Latin; and a broken clock–time never marches on in Lisbon. I see two lone water–splashed columns marking where a slip ends and a watery road begins. I need to follow the waterfront a little more.

Lisboetas jostle against me and each other converging on queues snaking from the ferry terminals. A group of conductors idly smoke by a gangplank and laugh at the folly of a middle–aged man in a tweed jacket accidentally–on–purpose bump into a much younger and firmer woman. He suffers the consequences of his uninvited advance: a shout and a withering stare. Everyone knows the rules: look, but do not touch.

My new friend Mário told me specifically last night to get to the third ferry terminal at a quarter to two; he'll pick me up and we'll go to the beach with his sister and boyfriend. Five minutes to go, a glance at my watch reminds me. Too bad I don't exactly know where we are to meet.

At the concrete quayside, a pretty girl catches my eye. Slender and gently curved, my eyes cannot help but follow her. She moves in a slow sway that could turn me quintessentially straight. As she enters the terminal just before the Navy docks, I realize I met her last night. She called her boyfriend Cupido. They kissed a lot. Each time I caught the smooth muscle of their tongues slipping past lips to the other's mouth, my heart sighed.

"Vanessa?" I ask, hesitantly tapping her on the shoulder.

With a bit of a start, she turns around and smiles.

"Hi. I was sitting across from you at the reception for the Akademya Lusoh–Galaktika at the Restaurante Califórnia."

She scans my face for a moment.

"How can I forget? You're Vanda and Mário's American. What'd you call yourself?"

"Pukiki. Luso–Hawaiian. Portuguese from Hawaii."

"Yes. That's the word. So funny."

After a light *beijinho*:

"Would you like some water? I'm going to buy some."

The brisk walk tempting fate in a shirt, tie and blazer has me pouring sweat.

"Yes, thank you," I respond slowly.

A discrete smile.

Sitting on the curb, we watch the cars go by. She's sensibly dressed in a maroon top that circles her neck leaving her back and midriff bare. Her jeans are molded to her hips; in comparison, I must look like an overdressed fool.

She lights a cigarette.

"Aren't you hot?"

"I guess so."

I smile sheepishly, and off goes the woolen sack jacket and tie.

"It's two, right?" I ask. "Where's Mário?"

"Oh, he's always a little late."

She half–consciously blows smoke to the breeze.

Tapping a pack that reads Português Suave, she gestures for me to take a fag. Deco lettering and a building decorate the pack; blue and white vertical lines evoke the sea; the beyond. Cigarette between my lips, her Zippo's butane cuts the air.

"That's a cool cigarette pack. That's the Tower of Belém?"

"Uh–huh."

For an eternal second, I notice a group of crows across the street bobbing their heads in the sunlight. I wish I had something to talk about besides cigarette pack designs; I'll content myself with watching Vanessa through the corner of my eye. I could have worse company.

"You always wear a coat?"

Forgetting myself and context, I sigh and answer in English:

"Not always. I was at a conference this morning that was on aspects of the history of the Portuguese presence in the Indian Ocean. The seminars I attended were about the Portuguese expansion vis–à–vis the cultures they encountered. I think it was called 'Culturas do Índico.' It was put on by FLAD; the Luso–American Foundation for Development. I bugged–out early to be with you guys."

She looks at me a little blankly.

"I wanted to look nice for everyone."

"I don't follow. You should speak in Portuguese. When I'm in another country I always make an effort to speak the local language. You should, too."

"Oh I'm sorry. I forgot myself."

Vanessa smiles at me as I switch to Portuguese.

"*Tá bem.*"

"That's more like it."

"You said other countries?"

"Uh–huh. I've been to Morocco, France, Spain, the Netherlands…"

"Never England?"

"You interrupted me. I want to go to school there. To The Slade."

"My apologies."

I feel like such a cad.

"That's a museum?"

"The Slade School of Fine Art. It's hard to get into; I hope my portfolio is good enough."

"Oh."

My mind draws a blank. I want to say something about talent, but words escape me. I'm looking at her neck; her eyes catch mine. She looks up and starts waving to the street.

"Hey, look there's Mário, right on time. Almost."

Mário pulls up, all smiles and bursting with energy. His *namorado*, Fernando, is waving us in. I can't help but smile, too, when I get in the car. All of them have an alluring glow and Latin beauty. I feel lucky to be in such beautiful company. I wonder if they feel the same about me.

The car speeds like a bat out of hell past the avenues and squares I'd "toured" earlier this afternoon. Going up a narrow cobblestone street high above the city, Mário asks me if I'd like to go to a *festa*—a festival—with him, Fernando, his sister and Vanda. He chirps I have only five minutes to decide since we're close to where he has to buy the tickets. "We're going tonight," Vanessa adds. "It'll be the best," Fernando announces.

"Last night Vanda said that she's going with the film school. I'm invited?"

"Come on, man. Of course."

"*Oquei*. Well here we are."

As soon as my lips say sure and cash passes from wallet to insisting hand, Mário's out the door.

"It's in Albufeira." Vanessa sighs.

"I'm not too good with my Lisbon neighborhoods. Is that near Oerias?"

"No, man," Fernando laughs. "South Portugal."

"Algarve."

"What?"

"It's cool. We have a room with Vanda."

"We're heading out tonight?"

"That's what she said."

"Don't worry about it."

"But. I don't have any clothes with me."

"No man, when we're done at the beach, you can grab your clothes and things and we'll drive down."

"Is it far?"

"No man. Just head down the road for a few hours. Long beaches. White buildings."

"It's cool," Vanessa sighs again. "What's taking Mário so long? It'll be sundown by the time he gets back."

***

Driving over the 25th of April Bridge, Mário puts on something he calls *Pimba*, music for the Portuguese masses; he jokes he has an album or two out.

"Really?"

"Yes, I'm a really big hit with everyone."

"Right. So you're a call girl and a singer on the side?"

"Yes, that's me," he laughs and the accordion on the radio trills.

"Mário!" Vanessa shouts.

"Turn it off," Fernando groans.

"Only until the Caparica coast," laughs Mário.

We're following the heels of countless generations of Portuguese petite–bourgeoisie. Vanessa tells me they used to have a beach house out there when she was younger. A *barraca* or shack. You had a shack? A bright painted house; a cottage you'd call it, she says. She and her brother, she shouts, used to play in the sand for countless hours. Kicking sand at you, Mário shouts back. She used to bring her stuffed toys and give them shovels. I laugh, did they make sand castles together? Only the best, she replies. Our parents live in Almada now, closer to the beach and further from the dusty, expensive city. All I can say is oh.

I tell them I've heard the bridge having been called by many names. It depends on your politics, Mário tells me. The *Ponte Salazar, Ponte 25 de Abril, Ponte–Sobre–o–Tejo*. I translate and comment: Salazar Bridge, old school fascists. Not in vogue, says Fernando. 25th of April Bridge, today's name. Because of the Revolution. So, official name and commie pinko name? Yes, says Vanessa. And the Bridge Over the Tagus. That's what we, without politics call it, says Mário. It does describe it pretty vividly. Portuguese, says Vanessa, are a practical people. Our language reflects it. Like hummingbird. It's *beija-flor*. Kisses–flower, I say. Yes, says Vanessa. That's what it does. You might see some in the bushes near the beach, says Mário.

I'm imagining Mario and Vanessa sitting in the family car: he taciturn as she bounces and chants a song known to all children, dark eyes darting out the window and tender brown locks wisp in the breeze: "Papa, are we there yet?" Her father responds in the same practiced chorus: "No, dear, not yet." Mother quiets her with *limonade* and *sandes*. They're happy to be leaving the dusty city for an escape to the beach house. She has a small bear—Mr. Blue—tucked in her smock's pocket. Her hand goes down and gives his yarn–hair a squeeze. Mr. Blue's happy to be leaving Santana for long rolling evenings and sleepy dreams under a noiseless sky. She'll play with her cousin, pretending the vacant lot next to the villa is a desert and they'll be Arabs, in search of an oasis.

The Ponte–Sobre–o–Tejo is behind us; I look up at the red girders gleaming in the sun. Seagulls, the city's familiars, hover in broad arcs in a pristine azure sky around the spires of the bridge. I'm a paper airplane soaring in the sky, among the clouds and skirting the sun. Pausing a moment, I can hear the bridge's cables creaking. Somewhere there's a freighter's whistle.

"What was your happiest memory as a kid, out there?" I ask Vanessa.

"Father grilling sardines on an open grill."

"Don't forget the potatoes love, he'd always say to Mã," Mário says.

"Yes Mário. Remember the time you boiled the tomatoes instead?"

"Papa was so mad. And then he laughed. I heard wrong."

"I don't get it."

"You roast tomatoes, you don't boil them!"

"Oh, yeah. That'd be disgusting. With fish? Definitely."

"And," pauses Vanessa. "Steaks. Papa'd grill these wonderful steaks with eggs on top. They were wonderful. I miss those days."

She sighs and lights a cigarette.

I look out back over the bridge into the seemingly endless blue expanse of the horizon. Today's such a pretty day. The beach today. A festival tomorrow. Vanda tonight. Neat.

JENNIFER JEAN

Jennifer Jean is an American with both Cape Verdean and Azorean ancestry. Her debut poetry collection is *The Fool,*and her chapbooks include *The Archivist* and *In the War.* As well, she's released *Fishwife Tales*, a collaborative CD comprised of art songs, rock ballads, and accompanied recitations. Jennifer's next poetry manuscript addresses sex–trafficking issues in America. Her poetry, essays, and book reviews have been published in numerous journals, including: *Rattle, Waxwing, Drunken Boat, Poetica, Tidal Basin Review, Denver Quarterly, Solstice,* and *North Dakota Quarterly.* Her anthologized work appears in: *Veils, Halos and Shackles: International Poetry on the Abuse and Oppression of Women; Like One: Poems for Boston—The One Fund Anthology; Linebreak's Two Weeks; More Than a Number: Poems for Baga;* and *Mythology and Modern Women Poets: Analysis, Teaching, and Critical Reflection.* Her writing has received awards from the Academy of American Poets and from the International Seonghwa Poetry Competition. Jennifer is Poetry Editor for *The Mom Egg Review,* Administrative Editor for *Talking/Writing Magazine,* and she's an Associate Editor of *The Compassion Anthology.* She also teaches Free2Write poetry workshops to sex-trafficking survivors and she's on the advisory board of the Massachusetts Poetry Festival.

Human

There's no box
for Rose to fill
to register Mary.

In one hand she has Mary, rooting—
in the other a blue ballpoint,
hover–stuck
above the "Black" and the "White"
boxes. Rose writes through them:
"American." But

New Bedford
City Hall doesn't take that
kind of explanation. *Mary doesn't exist,*

laughs Vovó Linda
pinning a diaper on her grandchild,
while Rose fingers the City Hall
"resubmit form"
and considers writing "Green."
She writes "American," again. And weeks later it's
"American," again.

Till a knock comes
and Rose is handed the form.
"Human," she writes.
The man shakes his head.
We're Cape Verdean, she shrugs

as he rises from the armchair, and
looks at her, at Vovó,
at curly Mary—just small
enough for a breadbox.

They all shine like molasses.

He writes, "Black."

Dexter Asylum, Providence, RI 1932

Suppose Anna Mello died in a "maniac cell"
the morning of the last day, which is the third day
in the Dexter Asylum. Was she
bent with milk for the dead? Could she know
he was dead? He

might as well have never lived. Once, she was a stone
on the deck—blinking at the constant
sight of the sea
after the white and red Azores port of
Angra do Heroismo slid into the past—
that was 1910.
Just before the mainland monarchy fled Lisbon
forever. Her mother would have swallowed her bile
and slapped her girl, *Anna!*

Anna! The sea was the cell then. And later
the baby, the babies—the cell. Then the cell was
the dark sea, and the silence
the crying. Her mother was gone,
couldn't tell her, *Ha Mouro na costa...*
couldn't slap her awake, keep her
from that *negro* Diogo Mello,
from baby after baby
named Walter Joseph Elizabeth Alice then

the hungry one
who had a name that died with him like a conjoined twin.
And here, at Dexter, they made her
wash ten minutes before each meal—
like it mattered. They couldn't keep her

from the inner terrain of the Dexter wall
nearest the dairy on Asylum grounds. She had likely started towards the
cows

with a pail—but they would moo. So she *mooooo*
mooooo mooooo—ed

forever. *Lady, you're crazy!* shouted the sane, the captive
debtors running from Anna
to get the "maniac guards."
Maybe she ran then too, and battered her head
against the wall. She saw blood on the stone, asked,
Did Diogo put you there?

The Wall

*Of course children loved it—you "weren't anybody" until
you'd walked its entire length—but many learned the truth
about stone walls and poison ivy shortly after a triumphant
circumnavigation of Dexter Asylum. ~from the city of
Providence RI website*

He didn't even let her in.

Her grandson paid the taxi, told her, "Next time. Call first."
Then Alice was driven from his flat, down Hope Street,
to the nearest motel.

But this was it! Her one addled act.
Her mind had held. (And would hold
till she allowed pneumonia to take
her grip
and, in a *morna*, lead her to

her mother…) But this was it. Today—
a late afternoon whisper

had drifted over infomercials
as she sat and bent and furled a knee–high nylon.

This trip was meant to be an answer to that quiet: "Alice?
Alice?" that meant, "Visit Billy…
at Brown University…" *Did something get lost
in translation?* she wondered as they slowed in traffic,
as she toyed with the cab window. Out the window

was the old Dexter Wall she wouldn't climb as a girl. "Alice!

Alice!" some girls had yelled, in 1934 or 1935,
when walking the wall. "We'll meet you
back here…" They trailed off and little Alice, near their stolen ladder,

had faced the empty street.
Choked on the air.
Leaned on the wall. It was thick and

rough like a guardian angel.

She counted some *mooooooooooooooooos*,
though they couldn't be as close
as they sounded. Though they turned the Dexter dairy cows into mothers

and she didn't want to think about that. About her mother,
Anna, corralled into the Asylum…her *mamãe*

who used to say, "*Você é minha vida…*"
but to each child separately, secretly,
so that it had no meaning, so that she had no life. Anna had
too many words for kinds of love—
like *saudade* and *sedu,*

but Alice doesn't know what they mean any more. She'd lost
her Portuguese

by the time her old bones entered the taxi,
by the time she opened the window and heard a soft
moooooooooo

drifting up from the nothing behind the Wall.

ESMERALDA CABRAL

Esmeralda Cabral still considers herself a hyphenated Canadian forty years after leaving her home island of São Miguel in the Azores. She writes creative nonfiction and is currently working on a series of family stories. Her work has been published in newspapers, magazines and anthologies and two of her stories have aired on CBC Radio. Esmeralda is a graduate of The Writer's Studio at Simon Fraser University in Vancouver, Canada and she was a participant in the Disquiet Literary Program in Lisbon, Portugal in 2012.

A Hard Landing

I saw my father cry once, when I was seven years old. Tears were unusual in our house—my father was a quiet man who seldom raised his voice or showed much emotion. My mother too, rarely allowed herself to shed any tears. All my life, I'd known her to have an obsessive fear of death and sadness. She didn't like the colour black, or chrysanthemums or rosemary or candles or graveyards or sad songs or anything else that could remotely be associated with funerals, death or sorrow. If she ever saw a hearse on the road, she would come home, have a shower and change her clothes. In casual conversation, if the words 'death' or 'coffin' came up, she would get up immediately and wash her hands.

My mother never talked about death—not since her own mother died prematurely, at the age of 56. Since that happened five weeks before my mother's wedding, and long before I was born, death was a forbidden subject at our house from the time I can remember. There were no faded, framed pictures of our ancestors on our walls. If my father ever needed to go to a funeral, he would slip out of the house without my mother's knowledge or tell her that he was going for a coffee and it was understood between my sisters and me, that my mother was never to know where our father had really gone.

So perhaps my mother had wanted to protect me from sadness and that's why she didn't tell me that my father was crying that day because his father had died, in his sleep, sometime in the middle of the night. I remember following my mother around, pestering her to give me more information.

"*Mamã*, why is *papá* crying?
"*Vovô* is in the hospital."
"What's wrong with him? The doctors will make him better. Why is everyone so upset?"

I needed to reassure my father with my logic and went to his bedroom to look for him. The light was on but he was in bed, lying on his side, his back towards the door; the covers right up to his shoulders. I could see the back of his head with his prominent bald spot. The hair around it was tousled and sweaty. I tiptoed in, then jumped onto the bed, sat behind him and poked him gently in the shoulder several times.

"*Papá, o que é?*" Daddy, what's wrong? "*Vovô* will be okay, you'll see."

My father sobbed. I jumped over him, sat facing him and crossed my legs.

"*Papá.*"

My father looked at me, his blue eyes rimmed with red.

"He died, didn't he?" I asked.

My father didn't answer but his silence told me that my hunch was right. My grandfather was gone. I felt sadness and anger at once and all I could do was yell out "I want my *Vovô!*" Then I hugged my father, buried my face in the crook of his neck and sobbed. "Why did you lie to me?"

We were new immigrants to Canada, having arrived in Edmonton only five months before, in September 1969. All four of us, my mother, my father, my sister Maria and I, still had etched in our minds the image of my grandparents leaning out the window, waving good–bye as *Senhor Arturo's* car pulled away, carrying us and our luggage, inching slowly down the road at first, then picking up speed, finally ripping us away to the airport. All the neighbours were at their windows to wave good–bye to us.

"Look back three times," my mother said, "that way you'll be sure to return."

I looked back six times before we turned the corner; I wanted to double my odds. For my grandparents, watching their only child and his wife and children drive off like that—practically the whole family at once—must have been overwhelming. Yet it had been my grandfather's idea, I was told, that my father apply to emigrate and try to build a life in the New World.

Whenever I asked my parents why we were doing this, why we were rushing off to Canada like this, my mother would explain that she and my dad wanted to provide an education for Maria and me, just like they were for Antonia, my oldest sister, who was already pursuing her studies on Portugal's mainland.

"There's a university right in Edmonton, your uncle says." My mother was comforted by this fact and excited about the prospect that her daughters could live at home and go to university. My mother's brother had emigrated and settled in Edmonton and now he was sponsoring us.

"You girls won't have to leave home, we won't have to pay for your boarding, and tuition is so much cheaper," my mother reasoned. I hadn't even started school yet but I already knew that I would be going to university, that I wouldn't have a choice, since this upheaval the family was enduring was mostly for my benefit and Maria's too.

I found out many years later that my father's tears on the day his father died were about more than just grief. They were about helplessness. Twelve days after our arrival in Edmonton, there was a falling out between our family and my uncle's family, for reasons I still don't fully know or understand. We left my uncle's suburban home and found ourselves living in a large and practically empty house in Edmonton's inner city, in the heart of the Portuguese community. We had neighbours we could speak to but we were feeling lonely in this new and strange place. My father was earning minimum wage and my mother was not yet working; paying rent for the house was unexpected at that point and was a huge financial burden.

When my grandfather died, my father wanted to attend the funeral. It was not going to be possible. My parents had very little money and they had not planned to fly back home so soon after our arrival. When we found out the price of a plane ticket home, my father resigned himself to not attending his father's funeral—it was not going to be possible. My parents had no credit cards, no credit rating, and no way to borrow money. In the chaos of grief, my mother had thought it possible and sent a telegram home, asking the priest to wait a few days for the burial, that we were trying to arrange for a flight for my father. But she knew it was a long shot—their options were limited.

After watching my father's inconsolable sadness, my mother dressed in her winter coat, put on her boots, gloves, hat and scarf, because it was February, and February in Edmonton can be very cold, the kind of cold that forms icicles on your eyebrows and eyelashes after only a few minutes outside; the kind of cold that makes it painful to inhale deeply because your nose hairs have all frozen. My mother walked down the block to the home of another Portuguese family, people we barely knew but who might understand the anxiety of wanting to go home and not being able to. I went with my mother because I wanted to be there too. I wanted to be part of the solution to my father's grief.

Our neighbour's daughter, Alexandrina, worked at a bank downtown. My mother explained the situation and asked her how we could borrow money for a plane ticket for my father. She said that there was no way any bank would lend us that kind of money but, after conferring with her mother in another room, offered to personally lend my parents the money. The ticket was purchased the next morning and soon after that, my father was on his way to Toronto, then Montreal, then Lisbon and then the Azores. By the time he reached São Miguel, it was too late, his father had been buried. The message hadn't arrived in time that my father was on his way.

Three years later, when we were firmly ensconced in our new country and growing familiar with Canadian culture, we sponsored my grandmother and she came to live with us. I loved having her in our house; she was a storyteller and I couldn't get enough of her stories. When she got ready for bed and started brushing her beautiful, silver hair, one–hundred strokes every night, that would be my cue to go into her room and ask her to tell me about the old days, about the old country.

"Well, what do you want to know today?" she would start, and then keep going without waiting for my answer. "Let me tell you about my *Avó Paulina*. She was a very strong woman—why she raised my mother all by herself—and then she came to live with us when I was a baby. She was well respected, a good woman. When I was older, she used to braid my hair, one long, thick braid, down my back."

At that moment, I remember touching my head and my very short hair, and wishing it was long and silky so that my grandmother could braid it for me too.

I was fascinated by my grandmother's stories. She was not afraid of death like my mother was, so she could tell stories about the people in my family who had died—people I hadn't known but wanted to hear about. I lapped up her stories and begged for more.

"No, no more tonight. I have to go to bed. And so do you! Go on, we'll talk more tomorrow."

My grandmother was a large, heavy–set woman. She wore black, of course, as did all the Portuguese widows in those days, and to my surprise, my mother accepted this without question. There was never any mention that my grandmother was a grieving widow. In fact, it had been my mother who had insisted that my grandmother join us in Canada, and then worked through all the red tape to help her obtain her immigration papers. She did not want my grandmother to live out her last years alone, far from the only family she had. The two women had not always had an easy relationship, often competing for my father's attention, but age and circumstance had mellowed them both and they became not only in–laws but friends too.

Weeks after my grandmother's 87th birthday, she developed pneumonia, was admitted to the hospital and died several days later. I was 19 years old. When the phone rang and the nurse told me that my grandmother had passed away, I had to break the news to my father.

"Daddy," I began after I hung up the phone.

"I know, I know. You no have to say nahting," my father said.

"We have to go to the hospital, Dad. A family member has to sign papers."

He looked at me with his blue, teary eyes and said, "You go, *filha*. I no can do that. I going cry."

My mother went to my grandmother's funeral but kept a slight distance from the gravesite at the burial. As the coffin was lowered into the ground, my mother walked away and headed back to the car. I watched her through the crowd and I could tell from the way her head was bowed and her shoulders were scrunched near her ears that she was crying.

When we got home, my father sat at the kitchen table and poured himself a shot of Port. I noticed that he brought out the special Port—the one that he reserved for special occasions, not the regular, cheaper version that we would splash into the fruit salad for a bit of extra flavour at dessert. My mother sat at the table, held her head in her hands and said, "She was my best friend." Then she got up, had a shower, changed her clothes and started to get dinner ready.

JOÃO S MARTINS

João S Martins, 59 years old, was born and raised in Manteigas, Portugal. He earned his degree at the Catholic University of Lisbon. During his time in Portugal he dedicated himself to teaching and education at various levels of public institutions. He first arrived in the U.S. in 1986. Even though he had plans of only staying a month, he decided to relocate to the U.S. permanently with his family. He has resided in Livingston, NJ for the past 24 years. He has published 7 books: "Exercício de Pintura"—*Exercises in Painting*—poetry; "A Estrelinha da serra..."—*The Little Mountain Star*—short stories; "Cânticos Paralelos"—*Parallel Chants*—poetry; "Intervalo das Palavras"—*The Space Between Words*—poetry; "Quando toda a esperança é azul"—*When All Hope Is Blue*— biography; "O seu nome era Maria"—*Her Name Was Maria*—illustrated poem; and "mãos verdadeiras"—*Truth in Hands*—poetry. He's also been honored with publication in numerous online and local publications and is a member of the Portuguese Writers Society. As founder of ProVerbo—a cultural arm of the Portuguese Sport Club of Newark—he's organized cultural galas as well as poetry events, among other cultural club activities. He's a fan of Portuguese music, painting, and all arts in general. He's recently dedicated himself to the craft of wood carving. He writes for a blog focused on the arts and his wood carving projects (artamarte.blogspot.com).

vice–versa

chegará sem dúvida o momento
inevitável em que eu ou tu estaremos
na sala sós olhando literalmente
para a janela uma das muitas janelas
de ontem ou do amanhã entreaberto

e eu lerei para ti ou alguém virá ler
para mim a tua carta ou um qualquer jornal.
a voz será mais importante e suave
que as notícias ou os resultados
dos políticos ou dos concursos desportivos.

se for dia dos teus anos cantarei
ou se for o meu aniversário dirão
parabéns (pela longa vida?) por tudo
quanto a idade permitiu fazer
ao longo dos dias de inverno mais curtos.

é esta regra até aqui universal
pelo menos assim nos ensinaram.
quem sabe poderemos mudá–la
pelo menos não nos faltará vontade
e coragem mas as forças... nesse dia

seja depois de te ler o teu livro
preferido ou te lavar as mãos
ou de alguém me cantar felicidades
ou provar o bolo e soprar as velas
sem apagar da memória os outros

muitos anos de nós dois que estão
presentes em cada gesto em cada olhar.
a tua mão afagará a minha e eu a tua
deixaremos que as mãos falem
enquanto o olhar vigia no longe. qualquer

que seja o lado da sala o eco dos afectos
condensados e as palavras uma ou duas
—filho mãe – ou três ou tantas muitas
memórias. fomos parcos de palavras
talvez nem façam tanta falta

agora que ainda nos temos. depois…
vamos cortar só para nós dois o bolo e
saborear. tu lês e eu escuto e num sorriso
dirás para mim parabéns e eu direi
muitos anos de vida. adormeceremos

ou vice–versa…

Vice Versa (Trans.)

the inevitable and unquestionable moment
will come, you and I in the living room,
alone, looking at the window in front us,
one of the endless windows of yesterday,
or the half—open tomorrow.

and I'll read for you, or someone will read
me your letter or any other paper.
the voice will be sweeter, more important
than any breaking news,
political debate or score of a game.

if it is your birthday I'll sing, or
if it is my anniversary they will say:
congratulations (for your long life) for
everything the years allowed you to do
during the winter days, shorter and shorter.

this is the rule so far universal
at least the way they taught us.
who knows if we can change it,
if we wish and if courage does not
abandon us, as the strength… on that day

after I read you your preferred
book or I washed your hands, or
after they wished me good luck,
or blew out the candles and tasted the cake…
without being erased from my memory

so many years of the two of us,
presents in every single gesture and regard,
your hand will caress mine and I yours
let our hands do the talking when
our eyes are vigilant looking into the distance.

doesn't matter the room, the echo
of condensed feelings flies free, the words,
one or two—son—friend—or three, or
so many memories. always short of words
maybe we don't need them now

that we still have each other. later …
we will cut the cake just for the two of us and
will taste it. you read, I listen and, smiling,
you will say: happy birthday and I will say
many many more. then we will fall asleep

or vice versa…

almanaque dos escritores

na rádio um poema lido
com voz intimista de circunstância:
dois colegas de escola
este bom em matemática literatura
filosofia poesia e outras artes
visuais e auditivas
terra a terra sensíveis.
aquele dedicado à ciência física
e química com apetência para outros voos
menos íntimos pouco lúdicos
nada estéticos.

aquele publicou textos
e cartas de amor com o mesmo intervalo
com que o segundo oferecia
bombas de misericórdia
assim ele dizia os útimos desejos
vistos lá do alto aos que num ápice
iriam ser sacrificados em nome
de uma ideia uma cultura um deus.
o dele
nunca o deles. alucinação
contagiante fantasia egocêntrica

nadava o primeiro entre livros
e folhas de água calma no lago
repousado de orlas claras
em balanceadas linhas sensíveis
cores de repouso e criação
alheadas das outras cores
de fogo sons relâmpagos
explosões de terror insensível
às erupções interiores
das consciências

parei o carro à beira da estrada
desliguei o motor e entrei
neste pequeno oásis de tempo
sem muros. só os desenhos
no jardim canteiros e arbustos
continuei a escutar ...

entre dois lados contrários
há sempre um terceiro ponto de vista:
chamar–lhe–ão alguns verdade
direi talvez: caminho. o meu.

e todos os dias às sete horas
e trinta minutos de cada tarde
a mesma voz circunstancial
alinha datas recorda efemérides
e lê um poema
um entre muitos que eu gostaria
ter escrito
no almanaque dos escritores

quero escrever um texto livre
em que ele próprio livremente
diga o que ele sente e eu sinto
sem me prender inutilmente
ou eu nele me sentir preso
ou dependente
que me respeite saia mundo fora
e bata de porta em porta
entre de casa em casa
livremente para ser lido

the writers almanac (trans.)

on the radio a poem is read
in an intimate and fortuitous voice:
two friends from school
one good in mathematics literature
philosophy poetry and other
visual and auditory arts
sensitive and down to earth.
the other devoted to physics
and chemistry with a liking for other flights
less intimate a little less playful
not at all aesthetical.

one published texts
and love letters with the same frequency
the other offered
mercy bombs
so he said the last wishes
seen from above to those whom at an eye's blink
would be sacrificed in the name
an idea of a culture a god.
his
never theirs.
contagious hallucination egocentric fantasy

the first one was swimming among the books
and pages of still water in the peaceful
lake of clear bounds
in balanced lines sensitive
colors of repose and creation
remote from the other colors
of fire sounds lightning
outbursts of senseless terror
to the interior eruptions
of consciousness

I stopped the car by the roadside
turned off the engine and entered
this small oasis of time
without walls. only the drawings
in the garden flower beds and shrubs
and kept listening ...

between two opposing sides
there is always a third viewpoint:
some will call it truth
I might say: path. mine.

and every day at seven
thirty each evening
the same fortuitous voice
aligns dates recalls events
and reads a poem
from the almanac that I would have liked
to have written
in the writers almanac

I want to write a free text
expressing itself freely
what it feels and I feel
without me becoming needlessly attached
or feel trapped
or dependent
to respect me and depart
to knock from door to door
from house to house
to be read freely

JOE AMARAL

Joe Amaral splits his time spelunking around the California central coast as a paramedic and stay at home dad to two saucy little girls. He was born and raised in Hayward. His poetry and short stories have appeared in many awesome places around the world. Joe won the 2014 Ingrid Reti Literary Award. He has also hiked Mount Kilimanjaro, taken language lessons in Lisbon and explored Machu Picchu.

The Invisible Minority

My mother is one hundred percent

Portuguese

descended from the Azores Islands
In grade school she was considered

Hispanic

Lumped as a minority
and treated as such

When I applied for colleges
I proudly/jokingly
stated my ethnicity as

Other: Azorean

I was categorized

White/Caucasian

a generation later despite
being a pure–blooded Portagee

Apparently my immigrant status
joined the

British

and

Irish

and

Italians

who created the first ghettoes
and forgot the new life opportunity
their ancestors eked out for them

My great–grandparents died

in their thirties as slaves to Massachusetts
cotton mills–nobody lasted
more than eight cancerous years
before their diseased lungs filled up with fluid
and drowned them

My grandparents spoke our native tongue fluently
My mother too– but then she was told
only to speak English in school
Mom completely lost
the Portuguese language
she was born and inherited into

I only experienced my culture
in snippets and short stories
from the age–burned scroll
of my sheepherder grandfather's memory

I am foreign the way food may be spicy
Not red hot, not even medium
I am mild salsa, maybe a hint of fire

I struggle with my perceived
social status, my class allotment

But I refuse to fall under
an all–inclusive Anglo banner
symbolizing anything but peace
or hubris, as if my being an entitled

White American

gives me the power
to pretend I am above
the poor races

who picked up the tools we dropped

Pa Pops

There is a time for everything, and a season for every activity under the heavens: a time to be born and a time to die, a time to plant and a time to uproot. —Ecclesiastes 3:1–2

He passed peacefully on an early spring afternoon,
his fruit trees in full bloom, his winter crops seeding
and his rows of fava beans ready for harvest

Ninety–five years old and bobbing
for apples in metal troughs

Some live a long life good enough,
others a good life long enough
Mel lived good and long

Dad, Papa, Pa Pops: Melvin Amaral was born in 1917 Oakland
He huddled in Castro Valley with family members
during the Depression, primarily raising chickens
and eventually building a poultry farm in Hayward
on an orchard full of apricot trees

It was on Meekland Estate property
with an eighty foot well from the Mount Diablo watershed
still running today with lots of care, oil,
and a gravity feeding tank house
He never tasted city water nor tested the well for chemicals

He trusted this earth to sustain him

Mel was an accomplished welder and inventor, turning
scraps of metal and old machinery into necessary equipment

He gathered seeds, tilled the land tenderly and knew how to reap
and provide for his family, share with his friends, and cook,

can, dry, juice and compost his fruits and vegetables
to utilize every shred of life

Mel married Mary Mendonca and they belonged to the
Pacific Growers Credit Union, and later the All Saints
Senior Center while watching their family grow and grow
like giant pumpkins and corn rows, combating the weeds
and other life obstacles in their way and succeeding

Mel and Mary belonged to Portuguese Lodges and camping
groups, loved to fish and smoke salmon in Fort Bragg,
clam on Pismo Beach, and travel the world, including the place
their parents immigrated from— the Acores Islands

They worked hard all day, but on the weekend, they danced

Isabel

Wandering narrow alleys in Bairro Alto
Treacherous cobbled pathways
Crookedly uneven curbs and haphazard hills
Darkling nights fading into pink dawns

She was a beautiful *bonita* Spanish girl
A chance encounter across two worlds
Morena tinge, chocolate hued
Fleecy tresses sweeping down
A loose ponytail spiraling askew

Slim of figure, short in height
White cloth slip on shoes
Bronzed eyes swimming in joy—
and sadness
A patchwork dress of blue

Loud laughs and broken English
Sometimes I'd speak too fast and mumble
She would stumble in drunken fluster
She loved her cigarettes a little too often
They affected her ability to climb the stairs of Alfama

Piggyback up the street in the starlit darkness
Lurching and cavorting until sunrise
Sleep completely forgotten
Put on hold until morning
The hours of night belonged to us all
A city alive and flaming

From afar we saw the river *Tejo*
Golden bridge beaming bright, sparkling water below
The roar of conversation and laughter
Music bouncing off the ancient walls
Smoke meandering aimlessly in the air

Drifting about like the people
In, out, everywhere

Lisbon, *Lisboa*
Careless, unhindered
Old World charm

At first sight I guessed she was Portuguese
Then she told me, *"Tem cuidado"*
She was right in that statement more than she knew
We enjoyed the company of many nationalities
connecting like fated friends are meant to do
A strong affinity of feelings
despite our vast differences

She is a big city girl who hates camping
and runs screaming from bees
I am adventurously the exact opposite
but life is different in our relative countries
Who is better off, one cannot debate– the same
food tastes good or bad on different trays

I never thought it would be hard to say goodbye
crossing that vast Atlantic Ocean a continent away
to someone you hope to see again but may never
due to conflicting circumstances–
life's twirling path

But my Spanish girl will always be remembered
A brief meeting, a big impact
una pequena menina to forever treasure

My true friend whom I will truly miss
I turn around for the last time
to blow her a final kiss

Hot Tub Time Machine

I scald in my hometown spa, post
gym and swim, looking up
at the square blue sky, restless
as an unfurled jean pocket reaching
from the floor in the stiff right
angles of American architecture,
two buildings smushed together
like the wrinkles on my fingers
and I wish I was in Portugal again

I change the stucco to cobblestones,
the unpainted concrete to *azulejos,*
the cinder blocks into castle walls–
Sintra, a palace out of *Fantasia*

The sky is a time warp. It stays the same

I wander *Lisboa,* buying cork tree products
and *bacalhau.* I think of earthquakes and fires
in 1755 Lisbon and 1906 San Francisco, their
rebirth, their sister bridges, feats of engineering

I surfed the topsoil in 1989
when my own temblor struck
during the Bay Bridge World Series

As I soak I dream of living two lives
simultaneously, across oceans, twin
cities reincarnated, and I realize I would only
compound my unease
double my aimlessness   and
yearn for even more nostalgia
than this time traveling hot tub nausea

AUGUST MARK VAZ

August Mark Vaz, (1926–2013), who spent his childhood on the island of Terceira in the Azores, was a pioneer in writing and lecturing about the Portuguese in America. *The Portuguese in California* is still cited as a valuable book, and he co–wrote *Cooking With a Portuguese Flavor* with his wife, Elizabeth S. Vaz. He was a beloved history teacher at San Leandro High School in the California Bay Area for over three decades as well as being a skilled painter and gardener.

Elizabeth S. Vaz resides in Castro Valley, California, where she raised six children and taught English at Holy Names College in Oakland. She co–wrote *Cooking With a Portuguese Flavor* with her husband, August Mark Vaz.

Cooking With A Portuguese Flavor
co–authored with Elizabeth Vaz

In the 1960s, my parents published a collection of the traditional recipes of Portuguese–American (mostly Azorean) culture. Some selections were prefaced by brief essays. A number of fine Luso cookbooks are now on the market, but theirs was an early exemplar and sold out several editions. It was lauded in not only the Portuguese press but in major newspapers in California, Massachusetts, New Jersey, and elsewhere. My father (his roots are in Terceira) was a pioneer in lecturing and writing about Luso culture, and his volume The Portuguese in California is considered by many to have paved the way for numerous other writers of Portuguese descent, including me. My mother worked hard to convert anecdotal material, and scrawled on inexact recipes, into standardized formulas, and she was a loving and devoted shepherd in the festivals and traditions of my youth.

–Katherine Vaz

LAND
One of the most famous Portuguese soups is the *sopas e carne* served at the celebration of the Holy Ghost, (*Festa do Divino Espírito Santo*), also called the Pentecost festival. While never canonically established, the *Festa* has remained a religious event since 1296, when Queen Isabel of Aragão, wife of King Diniz of Portugal, first offered a dinner in a spirit of charity and placed the royal crown on the head of the poorest citizen as an act of personal humility. She herself served the impoverished assembly.

The idea spread and was taken to the Azores by colonists; it was brought to America by Azorean immigrants. The *Festa* assumes a carnival air, with dancing (often the *chamaritta*, or Portuguese square–dancing) and parades. A caped Queen and her attendants are crowned. The highlight is the serving of the *sopas*, the communal meal.

The rich broth is accented with the green of the kale, and the distinctive mint flavor adds an unforgettable touch. An old custom is to add a teaspoon of wine (port is recommended) on top of your soup; mix in slightly.

SOPAS E CARNE
2 lbs. stewing meat
2 tablespoons oil
1 onion, thinly sliced
2 or 3 cloves of garlic
6 whole allspice
10 whole peppercorns

2 bay leaves
2 tablespoons vinegar
2 tablespoons brown sugar
1 small can tomato sauce
1 cup white wine
1 cup beef bouillon or vegetable stock
½ head cabbage, shredded/thinly sliced
4 cups thinly sliced kale
6 tops of mint stalks, roughly chopped

Brown the meat and onion quickly in the oil. Add the garlic, allspice, peppercorns, bay leaves, vinegar, brown sugar, and tomato sauce; sauté slightly and pour in water to cover. Simmer several hours, or until meat is tender.

Remove the meat and strain the broth. Recombine meat and broth and add the wine, bouillon or stock, cabbage, and kale. (Kale leaves can be stacked, rolled tightly into "cigars," and sliced as thinly as possible.)

Simmer until the vegetables are thoroughly cooked. Add mint and serve. Traditional serving includes ladling the soup over hardened (stale or dry) bread in individual bowls, or serve bread separately. Serves six.

SEA

The sea is the joy and sorrow of the Portuguese, for in giving life it also takes it. *Bacalhau* (cod) is the mainstay, but it is not the only resource from the fishing fleets that since time immemorial have gone out from the long coastline into the deep expanse of the Atlantic. *Varinas* (fishwives) carry their load of fish throughout the streets of Lisbon, and in the early morning they chant about wares ranging from common varieties of fish to lobster, prawns, clams, sardines, tuna, mussels, and octopus. The brightly–colored boats with their Phoenician–style designs set out in a daily exodus in the mist–filled dawn, while the *varinas* stand watching on the golden beaches—a ritual so old that people can easily find themselves dreaming of past ages as the hours pass slowly and the quiet tension mounts among those who wait for the return of the fleets from the pounding waters.

After witnessing this, it is easy to understand the high–pitched sing–song of the *varinas*, the slight swagger of their bodies as they wander the streets. Their pride elevates the meaning of what you buy: It is not only fish for food that you purchase but the heroism of men who went out to sea, engaged it, and returned with its abundance.

The *caldeirada*—or simply "kettle of fish"—is a traditional stew for fishermen and their families. Into a big iron kettle goes all sorts of seafood and whatever products of the land are on hand—onions, potatoes, bread, etc. Often the stew is made on the beaches when the fishing vessels return. The *varinas*, wrapped in shawls, have waited in hushed groups for hours.

Here are two versions; there are many. *Caldeirada* makes for a happy gathering: with a little imagination, you, too, can be on the beaches of Portugal.

CALDEIRADA À PESCADORA
1/3 cup olive oil
2 large onions, thinly sliced
1 large can of stewed tomatoes, or about 4–5 medium fresh ones, diced
3 cloves of garlic
4 cups of water
½ cup chopped parsley
1 piece lemon peel (or about 1 tsp. grated)
1 piece orange peel (or about 1 tsp. grated)
½ teaspoon thyme
1 bay leaf
several filaments of pure saffron, or to taste
2 teaspoons salt
½ teaspoon pepper
2 teaspoons sugar
1 tablespoon flour (mixed with ¼ cup water)
2 lbs. halibut (or any other fish, or combination of fish)
½ lb. shrimp

Brown the onions in the heated oil. Pour off excess oil and add tomatoes, garlic, water, parsley, lemon and orange peels (or grated peel), thyme, bay leaf, saffron, salt, pepper, and sugar. Stir well and blend in flour that's been mixed with ¼ cup water. Simmer at least 30 minutes to allow the flavors to develop.

Add halibut or other fish and simmer 20 minutes more. Add shrimp and heat until the shrimp turns pink but is not overcooked. Remove whole orange and lemon peels, if used. Accompany the hot stew with French bread torn into hunks and placed in bowls or served separately. Serves six.

MÓLHO DE PEIXE
This Boatman's Stew may be made well ahead of time and improves with

reheating. The cubed potatoes may be boiled separately and added thoroughly cooked right before the stew is ready.

    ¼ cup olive oil
    2 large onions, thinly sliced
    2 cloves of garlic
    1 large can diced or stewed tomatoes (or 4–5 fresh tomatoes cubed)
    1 15–oz. can tomato sauce
    4 cups water
    1 cup chopped parsley
    1 cup white wine
    mint off 4 stalks, roughly chopped
    3 medium potatoes, cubed
    2 lbs. cod, halibut, or any combination of fish

Heat oil in a deep pot and sauté onions and garlic until softened. Drain off excess oil. Stir in tomatoes, tomato sauce, water, parsley, wine, and mint. Simmer 30 minutes. Add the cut–up potatoes and fish and cook slowly another 30 minutes, or until potatoes and fish are done. Salt and pepper to taste. Add more water to thin the stew further, if desired.

The traditional serving method is to ladle the stew over hard (stale) French bread in each bowl. You may have to add more water to have enough liquid to soak into the bread. Or serve bread separately. The mint adds a distinctive taste; don't be tempted to omit it! Serves four to six.

Whaling, Gold and Homesteading

(Excerpt from *The Portuguese in California*)

The Early Years

When the British captain Vancouver visited Spanish California in 1792 and anchored at Monterey, five or six men deserted. Life aboard a ship in those days was based on harsh discipline readily administered by the lash and the appeal to jump ship was a constant one. Three of the deserters, one Dane and two Portuguese, were apparently allowed to remain in California since they were not British subjects. While no record remains of the others, one of these men may have been the first documented Portuguese settler in California, Antonio Rocha, who first appears in the records the Los Angeles area in 1815.

What is known of Rocha is that he was born in Portugal and in 1815 arrived in Los Angeles, then a sleepy little Pueblo. By 1828 he had become the owner of La Brea, a vast spread of 4,600 acres. It was this first recorded Portuguese settler in California, who constructed the famous mill at Mission San Gabriel and who eventually built an adobe structure in the pueblo of Los Angeles (located at what was to become Court and Spring Streets). In 1853 this adobe was purchased by Los Angeles County as the site for the municipal government.

Rocha is credited with having established some of the earliest whaling stations in California. [4]

The earliest migration of the Portuguese to California was, in fact, largely due to the expansion of the whaling industry to the shores of California.

As early as 1780, a flotilla of some 200 whalers dropped anchor in the Azores to round out its crew with men from Faial, Pico, San Jorge, Flores and Corvo. Many of these ships later made their way to the eastern coast of the United States and to California, although we have no record to indicate how many men might have jumped ship and remained in either location.

After 1819, when the first whaling ship dropped anchor in the Sandwich Islands, Hawaii became a kind of international stopping place for whaling ships on their way to San Francisco, then known as Yerba Buena. When the impact of the Gold Rush of 1848–9 turned the Bay of San Francisco into a

---

[4] His son Antonio Jose Rocha, Jr. was born in Los Angeles in 1831 at the Rancho Rincon de Los Bueyes, or what is today Culver City. He served as district judge of Balboa from 1868 to 1873. The last descendent of Rocha was Antonio Ricardo Rocha born in Los Angeles in 1866, who died without heirs in January 1938 at the age of 72.

graveyard of abandoned ships, Honolulu became the main whaling center in the Pacific, transforming a sleepy little village into an international seaport. The search for whales took these early captains far out into the Atlantic, to the coast of Brazil, around the Horn and into the Pacific, and even into the Indian Ocean and the waters off Japan as well as to the Antarctic. Yankee ships from New Bedford, Massachusetts, often manned by an international crew, became a common sight in the ports of the Pacific.

Even before the Gold Rush, whaling began to lose some of its romantic appeal for Americans. American energy turned from the sea to the drama of the westward movement. The lure of land and adventure turned back the eyes of the young men to the vastness that stretched from the Pacific to the Mississippi.

By the 1830's it had become the custom for whaling ships to fill out the crew by recruiting Portuguese from the Azores. The Portuguese were noted for their seamanship, hard work and ability to spot the whales. In the 19th century, not only whaling ships but merchant ships made the Azores a stopping place. The reasons were very practical: provisions could be secured far cheaper than at home and ships about to head for the Horn often made it a point to touch at the Azores. The Azores represented a ready supply of willing labor, as we see from this magazine article of 1878:

> It was on July 23rd that the A–1 clipper bark *Jehu* sailed from Boston for Fayal and a market, in ballast. She had in the steerage thirty–one Portuguese, who were returning home, and the object of the voyage was ostensibly to secure a charter for an early cargo of oranges in November, but really to obtain, clandestinely, a haul of Azorean passengers flying the islands in face of the stringent prohibitory laws against immigration. There is in the Portuguese dominions a strict system of conscription, under which every man, on reaching twenty–one, must incur the chance of being drawn for the army; and in consequence no one can leave the Azores who has not yet had his name shaken in the lot, unless he gives bonds in three hundred dollars that he will return and serve, if drawn, the money to be forfeited if he fails to respond, and this regulation applies even to mere lads scarce weaned...
>
> ... for years they have found means to evade the observation of the Government, escaping on passing whalers, whose crews are largely composed of Portuguese, or on English and American traders, which have occasionally cruised among the islands for the purpose of "stealing Portuguese," as the business is called.[5]

---

[5] I.S.G.W. Benjamin, *The Atlantic Islands as Resorts of Health and Pleasure.* (N.Y., 1878), p.33.

The *Jehu* under a Captain Brown was bound for Boston, having as second mate one Manuel described as, "very handsome, black–bearded, eagle–eyed, and with a herculean frame"; her entire crew was Portuguese.[6]

The description of the Azores, those mysterious islands jutting out from the sea between Europe and the New World, would be as descriptive today as it was then,

> ... impressive to observe how every available patch of earth is everywhere terraced and cultivated by man, who here seems fitted both with wings and claws to till the soil on its bits of slope, at an angle of sixty–five degrees, to the very edge of precipices that drop hundreds of feet to the ever–beating surge below.[7]

This was the vision: the carefully worked land and precious soil, which the immigrants from the Azores, bound across the sea, carried in their hearts and in their memory.

Many a Portuguese earned his way to the east coast of the United States, to Hawaii, or to California, by shipping out as a deck hand aboard these early whaling ships. The whaling ship was the early highway to the New World, and in the period from 1833 to 1863 unknown numbers quietly made their way to a new life.

By the 1850's whaling companies, largely Portuguese, were found at Half Moon Bay, Pescadero, Monterey, Carmel, San Simeon, Point Conception, Portuguese Cove and Portuguese Bend, as well as at San Diego. In 1850 one Antonio Vitorino was in charge of a building in Monterey which served as the Portuguese whaling station for that area.

At Point Lorna, the whaling industry lasted from 1868 until 1870, disappearing with the discovery of petroleum in Pennsylvania and in California.[8]

---

[6] *loc. cit.* The account also appears in *Scribner's Monthly* of September, 1873, and includes a more extensive description of the Azores at the time.

[7] Benjamin, *op. cit.* p.33.

[8] Early pioneers in this area were Manuel F. Cabral (1851), Francisco G. Simas (1861), both from Ribeiras, Pico. In 1874 one Anastacio (also from Pico), arrived in the area and in 1889 sailed for Mexico never to be heard of again. In 1874 we find Manuel Avila (who died off the coast of Chile in 1884); in 1874 from Faial came Joao Silva and in 1882 Manuel Machado Medina, the latter returning to the Azores in 1890. In 1882 came Manuel Silveira Soares (from Pico), Jose Soares Henriques and Jose Miquelino, all from Pico and all returning to the Azores in 1890. Arriving after 1884 (all from Pico) came Jose Moniz Medeiros, Manuel Francisco Avila, Jose Francisco Avila, Joao Garcia Tavares, Manuel Francisco Madruga, Manuel Francisco Avila, Joao Garcia Tavares and Jose F. Avila (the latter three left

As late as the 1880's, a whaling station was still located at San Simeon to spot passing whales going south in the winter or north in the spring, drawing Portuguese from the Monterey area for the seasonal occupation. This whaling station was the last operated by the Portuguese before the total disappearance of the whaling industry. The station had been established sometime in the early 1850's and here we find recorded some pioneers' names: Captain Jose Pedro, Captain Jose Silva and Captain Pereira.

At Pescadero the record shows a Captain Bennet, an anglicized version of Bernardo, while at Pigeon Point in Half Moon Bay there was a Captain White, whose Portuguese name before translation had been Alves.

By 1855, seventeen Portuguese whaling companies were found in the Monterey vicinity, busily engaged in processing whale oil. Within a three year period this Monterey group processed over 24,000 barrels of oil.

William Taylor in his *California Life Illustrated*, published in 1859, notes that:
> Fisheries are becoming a fruitful product of the California coast! A company of Portuguese in Monterey have gone into the whale fishery along the coast, and have taken from whales which they have captured since March, 1856, say eight months, sixteen thousand gallons of oil, which were sold for twelve thousand dollars.[9]

Quite a handy sum for those days! He also notes that there is extensive salmon fishing along the Sacramento, an occupation which naturally must have drawn many Portuguese.

In 1861 a small whaling operation was located at Point Lobos, at Carmelito Cove, run by some twenty Portuguese. Whales were sighted from "Whalers' Knoll" and brought into the cove where great iron caldrons were used to boil the fat for the whale oil. Nearby the whalers had their cottages and neat little gardens, where an old Azorean staple, the fava bean, was grown. This station was finally abandoned in 1884.

Even before 1850, Portuguese made their way into San Luis Obispo County, drawn by the whale industry in that area. One of the most prominent Portuguese whalers at the time was Captain Joe Clark, who in

---

California in 1891), Jose Moniz Madeiros (1884), Jose Muller (from Calheta) and Antonio Andrade (from Santa Maria). All were fishermen.
[9] William Taylor, *California Life Illustrated*, N.Y., 1859, p.259.

1869 built the wharf at San Simeon. The names Portuguese Flats and Portuguese Lane recall this early period. In May, 1960, the Portuguese whaling station at San Simeon became officially recognized as a State Historical monument, with a plaque (number 726), recording this early phase of the Portuguese.

After the passing of the whale industry, the Portuguese in this area, as in other parts of the state, turned to cattle and dairy ranching and fishing.

San Luis Obispo is still an active Portuguese center in which the I.D.E.S., U.P.E.C., U.P.P.E.C., and S.P.R.S.I. play an active role in the life of the community and keep alive the traditions and heritage of the early pioneers.

LARA GULARTE

Lara Gularte's poetic work depicting her Azorean heritage is included in a book of essays called *Imaginários Luso–Americanos e Açorianos* by Vamberto Freitas. Her work can be found in *The Gávea–Brown Book of Portuguese–American Poetry*. She was featured in the Autumn 2014 issue of *The Bitter Oleander* with an interview with Paul B. Roth, editor, and a selection of her poems. Gularte earned an MFA degree from San Jose State University where she was a poetry editor for *Reed Magazine*, received the Anne Lillis Award for Creative Writing, and several Phelan Awards. She was a 2nd prize poetry contest winner for *Empirical Magazine's* 2012 contest, and nominated by *Bitter Oleander Press* to Best New Poets 2010. Her work has appeared in such journals as *The Bitter Oleander*, *California Quarterly*, *The Clackamas Review*, *Evansville Review*, *Permafrost*, *The Water–Stone Review*, *The Fourth River*, *The Santa Clara Review*, and she has been published by many national and regional anthologies. Her poetry manuscript, "Kissing the Bee," is scheduled to be published by Tagus Press. She is an assistant editor for *Narrative Magazine*.

Bound

I found a ship bound for the old country, so I could travel back to a past I never lived, to the life of my great grandmother, the woman who started my story... I twisted her ring on my finger, and made a wish. At the altar I kneeled for prayer and host, asked for the body and blood, asked for the resurrection of her body. I wanted her whole again, so we could find our way back together.

Crocheted into the night my *bisavó* talked to me in my language that she couldn't understand, she told me she wanted to go home. A ghost ship docked. It sat silent in the black water and waited for us to board. Her body merged with mine. We returned.

The island she remembered was dressed in crags and calderas. She said to me in broken English that when the lava stopped boiling, fish came to the shore and asked to be caught. Her hand filled with sky, breakers flowered on the beach, stones showed their faces. She helped me understand the waves, close and far. Showed me how to pass through air, pass through water, and enter the salt.

Mrs. Madruga Prepares Her Granddaughter for Hard Times
10

Mrs. Madruga warns her granddaughter about the blurry sun, heavy and hungry, the scarred vegetables, the ragged turnips, and how the garden understands the natural cycle, the quiet of slaughter. She shows her granddaughter where to place the snares, to listen for the chuff of breath, how to get tender meat by relaxing the animal, stroking it from breastbone to pelvis till it slumps in her arms. She teaches her granddaughter how to kill, fast, painless, with the edge of an open hand striking a blow to the bones linking back to head; the snapped neck. She guides the chore of pulling out the shivering insides, the tug of soft pelt, quick cuts, each joint giving way under the knife, her blood soaked hands cleansed by lemon. All the cooking in one pot, herbs, and water, onion tears, green pepper, bones bumping bones, the wild taste of meat changing to something sweet.

---

10 First published as "Mrs. McGregor Prepares her Granddaughter for Hard Times," *The Bitter Oleander*, Vol. 16. Spring 2010.

Lost Currents

The sea, the sky,
the birthright of her being.
Stones that sound against water,
against stone, heart of stone.
How deep the stone's truth.

The passion of a rising tide,
wave, after wave,
of memory.
Dream eye of wave,
fish eye.

Her people mapping sea routes.
De Gama rounding the Cape
of Good Hope.
Lost, in the folds of dark sea,
exile of spirit.

Salt, the skin
of another life.
A thousand histories,
charts, scaled and starry
to steer by.

The White City

Above seven hills the sol star shines,
casts away shadow.
Wind carries time around, and past,
raises up dust.

When white Freesia leans
against stained glass,
the *fadista* sweeps heat
down the boulevards.

A glow seizes albescent patinas,
as specters buff the domed church,
and ethers rise up with fish–eyes.

The Tagus River brings home the lost ones
through wrack, and conch,
messages of salt.

On the Avenida da Liberdade,
people call out for Santo António,
discover lost things.

Find the Madonna down a quiet alley.
She stands on a gate,
uses aquamarines to cut the air,
then hems the sky with gold thread.

PAULO DA COSTA

paulo da costa was born in Angola and raised in Portugal. He is a bilingual writer, editor and translator living on the West Coast of Canada. paulo's first book of fiction, *The Scent of a Lie*, received the 2003 Commonwealth First Book Prize for the Canada–Caribbean Region, the W. O. Mitchell City of Calgary Book Prize and the Canongate Prize in Scotland for the title story. In Portuguese he has published two collections of poetry, *notas–de–rodapé* (2005) and *eco(lógico)* (2014). His poetry and fiction have been published in literary magazines around the world and have been translated to Italian, Chinese, Spanish, Serbian, Slovenian and Portuguese. His latest book of fiction, *The Green and Purple Skin of the World*, was released by Broadview Press / Freehand Books in 2013. As a translator paulo has brought to the English language readers a range of Portuguese poets including: Nuno Júdice, Al Berto and Daniel Faria. To the Portuguese language readers he has translated the Canadian poets: Margaret Atwood, Michael Ondaatje, Gary Geddes, Patrick Lane and Marilyn Bowering. *The Cartography of Being*, Selected Poems of Nuno Júdice 1976–2005 (2012) is his latest book of translations.

és a onda sonora
tacteias a profundeza dos sonhos
submersos pelos dias extintos

de olhos encerrados para balanço
conjugas os planetas e enumeras as estrelas
preferes esses dias que já não irradiam luz, noites
onde o microondas ainda não era pressentido

refugias–te no embalo
lacrimoso do pacífico
relembras a corrente do ventre

os sinos badalam
só te ajoelhas perante a terra e as ervilhas em flor

dentro da noite
sob o farol da lua danças com uma abóbora entre os braços

beliscas e acordas as favas adormecidas
para que saboreiem a doçura da tua língua e a ária da coruja

só te vestes para te demolhares na banheira
plantada sob a macieira para purificar uma ideia de civilização
que insiste em te ocultar dos pés ao pensamento

a luz do candeeiro de rua
dificilmente detecta
o corpo da mulher no seu trajecto para a ponte

apenas o seu cachecol de seda
esvoaça e emana um rasto de luz

mesmo a sombra lhe escorrega
do corpo como uma camisa de noite
enroscada aos pés
implorando–lhe que não

que braços não são asas

nem todos os teus dedos
são asas para o voo do beijo

que resiste descolar rumo ao destino
de lábios incertos

a imagem contém os traços
de tudo o que deseja morrer sem deixar rasto

alimenta o fascínio dos arqueólogos
por tudo o que desaparece sem história

LINETTE ESCOBAR

Linette Escobar is a Portuguese–American poet whose work has appeared in several literary journals including *Babilonia, Transfer* and *The Santa Clara Review*. In 2012, she was accepted and received support to attend the prestigious Squaw Valley Writers Conference. In the same year, she participated in the first Kale Soup for the Soul Reading and won a live writing competition at the Portuguese Artist Colony reading series. She is currently working on a memoir about her experiences working in Thailand as a tsunami volunteer.

Immigrant [11]

My father wakes me before
he combs his monster—under—
the—bed hair. My father
standing solidly like an Italian
sausage. He opens his red, green, gold
mouth. Mouth of the dried pimento
hanging near the curing linguiça,
mouth of the Nina, the Pinta,
the Santa Maria. His tongue
is the Portuguese flag telling me
it's time to pray. Tongue
of a guppy, tongue like my brother's
pop gun, subtitle tongue.
My father has
eyes of the stained glass
rosette in St. Chapelle. Eyes
of the Empire State building. Eyes
filled with the New York harbor
and its torch. My father with hands
round the rosary. His tsunami
hands, purple hands, Sistine chapel
hands, hands of clay, nails
and terra—cotta tiles.
My father with the voice
of the Ave Maria, of the matina. The voice of Hiroshima,
voice of being chosen last, voice of being
team captain, my father with the voice
of a cement mixer. Voice of the great
Amen. My father with feet of the Olympian
running around shells in Sarajevo, feet washed by God,
feet of the raped, feet of the Bosnian,
the Nazi, the Jew. Double boned feet. I am afraid
of my father's anger. My father with the anger
of a box cutter carried in the deep green pocket
of a drugstore stock boy. Afraid of my father
by the graveyard. Afraid of my father's
mourning. His scurvy mourning, mourning
of the Winchester Mystery House, coat hanger
mourning, the mourning of a comic strip

---

[11] First published in *Santa Clara Review*, Spring 1991.

character, mourning in ashes,
like the day after the fire,
my father's mourning like the glass
of Porto that spills late at night.

Legacy[12]

Avó Elisa pounds together blue
corn and gray fava beans into a warm
mush she makes just for me.
I remember her doing this long
before my brothers were born, before
my grandfather died. She always carried
this strength, belting out hymns like
"Ave Maria" for her silver
friends. "Elisa," they say,
"You sing so beautiful." It makes her
smile, a secret smile. The smile
she probably gave my grandfather at
13. Smile of the little girl becoming
engaged. Smile of the lady
who wishes she could read. Years ago,
we went to Bingo every
third Sunday. All the ladies
smelled like white
bath powder, Jean Nate in a round paper box.
Mrs. Silva, Mrs. Rosario, Mrs. Ponte,
they all brought zucchini
bread. All let me close the
"free space" for them. Sometimes,
I won doilies or crochet slippers.
Avó. would tell me to save them for my hope
chest. Then, my hope was
deeper than her basement filled
with wooden barrels of grandfather's
vinho and yellowed calendars of army
girls. Today, Avó's house is quiet
like her smile when she doesn't understand
the lady at the store and asks
me to tell her in Portuguese—the house,
quiet and lonely like the wax
that drips slowly down a burning red
votive candle in a Catholic church. They
used to tell me it meant God
was there, that candle, so I worried
all through Mass that it would

---

[12] First published in *Transfer*, Fall 1992.

blow out. I feel that way sometimes still
in the glow of Avó. Elisa's shadow,
watching her knit in my grandfather's old chaise
recliner. She knits together oceans
that are all red and green and gold,
knits together the voices of
my great grandmothers and children
who never wore bandages no matter
what country they were calling home.

Family History Of

Sometimes I want to slip my skin off
easily as the skin
slides off purple grapes bleeding
into red wine.
Avovo stomped them
in weathered wooden barrels
until they became *vinho*
to drink with dinner,
with company, in jar glasses.
Memory seeps in flooding
through burlap
that he tied at the end of a garden
hose to plug up the gopher's hole.
I stopped moving the hoses
when he started using the machete instead.
Of Avovo I remember
little white pills to take
with boiled egg,
sound of spoon
cracking the shell,
that it was always Grandma who drove.
I don't remember
a party without *carne de espeto* roasting low
on metal poles, can smell
bay leaves as they were crumpled
on the meat while it was still blood.
There was that red quarter
Avovo gave me to put in the bank,
to become *rica*. I was rich,
told Mom it was a buffalo nickel
or an Indian head, something valuable
I thought. My mom taught me
every word of the song Avovo slapped her for singing.
When my cousin, Tony, and I screamed
about the lizard, Avovo chopped it
in half, in thirds,
the three parts were moving,
couldn't understand why they thought they were living
didn't notice they'd lost their head
and all the parts kept moving.

Rua de Cima

Here is the woman who walked into the sea
aqui está a mulher que entrou no mar
Here are rosary beads paint worn away
aqui estão as contas de um rosário com a tinta já que desapareceu
Cut open my spleen
Rasgame o tédio
Find what is left of the white house
descobre o que resta da casa branca
Walk to the armoir covered in dust
pigeons resting on top
Vai até ao armário coberto em pó
Pombos poisados no cimo
Find a lock of blonde hair
wrapped in tissue
descobre um carcacol de cabelo loiro enrolado num embrulho em papel
Find the black scarves
descobre os lenços negros
Black as tilled earth
Black as bile
negros como a terra lavrada
negro como a bílis

Here is the trunk of a man
who never became a priest
aqui está o tronco de um homem
que nunca se tornou padre
here is the trunk of a man
who never was a boy
aqui está o tronco de um homem que nunca foi criança
here are the blue hydrangeas
the belt that beat the children   the green
of kale in watery soup
Aqui estão as hortências azuis
o cinto que bate nas crianças, o verde
da couve na sopa aguada
here are the women
who didn't marry   the men who built
bridges   the whale teeth
carved into lace
aqui estão as mulheres
que não casaram os homens que construíram

189

pontes o dente da baleia
talhado em renda
here are the scales left unbalanced by mud
aqui estão as pratos de balança desreguladas pela lama
a minha casa é um sítio onde nunca vivi
home is a place I've never lived
encontra–a aqui no meu desassossego
find it here in my disquiet

A Definition

Avó Maria's house was falling. The earthquake had hit Faial a few years before leaving her house near collapse. Avó was dead. She died before the earthquake. She died before her body. When I saw her in Lisbon for the last time, the only thing I recognized in her eyes was the watery blue color she had passed on to me.

A blank book came in the mail, and all I wanted to do with it was write a letter to my tribe and confess that I am illiterate in my first language.

The tsunami ruins in Khao Lak are all gone replaced with teak resorts facing the clear blue sea and small shops selling noodles, silk, hand–tailored suits, milky massages and Singha beer. When the shopkeeper smiles at me and says, "Welcome, welcome," I look up. In the corner there will be photos of grandmothers, babies, daughters. There will be fruit and incense burning. Most foreigners do not look up. The brochures call Thailand "the Land of Smiles."

Here's the truth. The last time I had been at Avó's house I was a little girl. There was an abandoned store in the basement, and my brother and I played with the dusty scales. My brother wore a straw cowboy hat that said "Benfica" on it. We stayed out playing for long days, and I never imagined he would ever be sick.

I use the word tribe like we are some sort of family. However, some of you I have never met, and some of you I have had moments of wishing not to know.

The tsunami gave me tones I can mouth to say "I am fine," "Have you eaten rice yet?" The tsunami gave me a lover who carved my name into a coconut shell then had a baby with someone else. The tsunami gave me a friend who died in a motorcycle accident and children who will call me, *Sayama*, teacher, until I am old.

My Tio helped me up the rickety front stairs. "Cuidado." Be careful, he told me.

There was debris everywhere in Avó's *sala*. That was the room where I first saw a woman breast–feeding. My mom had to have a talk with me to explain it, as if it was something dirty. Now, there were pigeons nesting on top of Avó's armoir, and they flew away kicking up dust. I opened a drawer and saw Avó's linens, carefully, crisply folded.

My teacher said, "no one cares about your dear, dead grandmother." My friend Tony winced. This is my friend who hates the word *saudade* because everyone says it has no translation, then they translate it.

I can say in Thai, "Bad economy." I can say in Thai, "My heart is broken." I can tell my Tia in Portuguese all about meeting Jacinto Lucas Pires and discuss the movements in Portuguese literature related to the revolution. I can tell her about the friend I made in Portugal who grew up a mile away from me in California. When I want to leave her a note that I have gone for a walk, I sound out the words. Then I draw a foot just to make sure.

I have said, "I missed you" when the correct words would have been "I love you."

I was speaking English.

I went into Avó's house for the first time since she had died, but after the earthquake, to take things. As I fingered locks of hair wrapped in embroidery and found boxes of sepia toned pictures, my Tio handed me some sewing thimbles. I looked at him and said, "*Por que?* why?" He said in a low voice, "She wore these on her body, on her fingers, next to her." I took one and put it on mine.

It still felt warm.

DINIZ BORGES

Diniz Borges was born in Praia da Vitória, Terceira, Açores. He immigrated with his parents to California at the age of ten. He holds a BA from Chapman University and an MA from California State University, Dominguez Hills. He is a Portuguese language teacher at Tulare Union High School and College of the Sequoias, Visalia. He has been an active member of the Portuguese–American community since the age of 18 when he began a Portuguese Language radio program. A contributing writer for several newspapers in the Azores and the Portuguese–American communities both in the US and in Canada. He is the coordinator of the literary page *Maré Cheia* and the Portuguese language television program *Os Portugueses no Vale*. He is on the Board of several Portuguese–American organizations in California and at the national level. Publications include: *America: O Outro Lado do Sonho*, Câmara Municipal da Praia da Vitória, 1997; *Uma Outra América*—Edições Salamandra, Lisboa, 2001; *Aflred Lewis: Escritor de Emoções*—Direcção Regional das Comunidades, 2002. *On a Leaf of Blue*— bilingual Anthology of Azorean Contemporary Poetry, U.C. Berkeley, 2003; *América: O Outro Rosto*—Edições Salamandra, Lisboa, 2003; *O Outro Lado da Saudade*—Institute for Azorean American Studies, 2005; A Década Perdida– Crónicas de Uma América Cinzenta; Letras lavadas, Ponta Delgada, 2012. He coordinated and wrote the preface for *O Meu Coração é Assim*, a collection of works by the Portuguese poet Álamo Oliveira, Câmara Municipal de Angra do Heroísmo, 2005 and *Nem Sempre a Saudade Chora*, anthology of Azorean poetry on the topic of emigration, Direção Regional das Comunidades, 2006.

My Azorean–American Journey

Meus Queridos Filhos:

I was thinking about how to explain to both of you why I ended up in this unique cultural position that you see your father daily. One who is a language teacher in the United States living, many times, the life of an *outsider*. Why, you might ask, do I continuously embrace a culture and an amalgam of traditions and beliefs that are considered different, strange even, in the "land of the free and the home of the brave?" Why do I persistently live my life between two cultures, two language, and two worlds? Why do I feel in the periphery of American society?

I obviously do not have the answers for all these questions. What follows, *meus queridos*, are only some humble, disordered thoughts about my Portuguese–American experience. Thus, here are an amalgam of contemplative points that deal with language, culture, democracy, exile, alienation, and acculturation. It is an honest attempt to explicate my feelings about a tumultuous, yet enjoyable journey in the American "melting pot".

Yes, I was ten when your grandparents decided to embark into an American pilgrimage. Amongst tears and agony, they left their parents, the security of their home and their friends, and boarded a TWA jet that took us from a tiny archipelago in the middle of the Atlantic, the islands of the Azores, to the "New Eldorado—the land of milk and honey." But, to us, America wasn't a total stranger. I remember sitting down with my grandfather, your great grandfather, Manuel Ferreira Lourenço and hearing some of the most adventurous stories about this far away and intriguing place called: *America*. An excellent story teller, avô Manuel Charuto (his nickname, partly because his dad smoked cigars) lived in California for eighteen years. It was here that he made his small fortune and returned to his homeland. He would talk about the vastness of a land that in his eyes never seemed to end. He would mention the transformation that he, and others, had to go through. To him, America was a place you went to make your fortune. A place you didn't go to stay. He would mention how some of his buddies had decided to settle and had changed tremendously. "They even changed their names," he would tell me with anguish. "If you stay for long you don't know who you are," he would say in a forceful voice, to anyone who would seek advice about immigrating to the United States.

Now grandpa never studied alienation or acculturation processes, but his eighteen years in California gave him a sense that in order to survive, one must be subject to a metamorphosis that strips you of your own, unique self–identity. And when the bags of clothes arrived from America (our relatives were generous with their old clothes) we would devour them like hungry cats. We were bewildered by the strange and exotic smells of America. And avô Manuel Charuto would caution: "be careful, it is like drinking wine," he would say, "if you have too much you lose your senses, you become someone you don't recognize." Without any formal education, avô Manuel knew the feeling of estrangement he lived while in the States and would tell us, with a lump in his throat: "I had to come back to the island, I didn't know who I was there." And when my mother, your avó Albertina, told him that we were immigrating to America, he lowered his head and said: "It is a land of many opportunities, but be prudent, don't stay too long—don't change." However to this day I still think that deep down avô Manuel knew that we would never return home, and he also knew that we would never be the same. He knew that we were going to change.

Entering an American school at the age of ten was an experience that has marked and stayed with me. It was my first empirical feeling with what *avô Manuel* had, so eloquently, talked about. I was in a strange setting, with people who looked different and talked a different language. There wasn't a bilingual education program. I was put side by side with students who knew the material and the language. I remember that for the first time in my life I didn't like school. I would go to sleep at night hoping that I would awaken next to avó Leonor (my maternal grandma, who lived in our house) in the Azores. In my homeland I had been in school for four years, and although here I was put in the fourth grade, I felt like this was my first encounter with education. For nearly six months, until I began to grasp the language, I felt like a true stranger: labeled as different, rejected, misunderstood and stupid. At ten I didn't comprehend what it was like to live a complete life on the hyphen. And I didn't know that as Oscar Handlin wrote:

> The life of the immigrant was that of a man diverted by unexpected pressures away from the established channels of his existence. Separated, he was never capable of acting with the assurance of habit; always in motion, he could never rely upon roots to hold him up. Instead he had ever to toil painfully from crisis to crisis, as an individual alone, make his way past the discontinuous obstacles of a strange world. (Handlin, 271)

As time passed my alienation also transformed from an outer into an inner stage. I was now in my rebellious teenage years. I saw myself as an all American teenager and didn't want to associate with my Portuguese roots. The isolation I had felt during my childhood was now transformed into total assimilation and a dislike for any association with my community and my countrymen. I felt that in order to be American I had to abdicate my cultural ties to the country, and the people, I had grown up with. I wasn't about to feel like a marginal member of society, ever again. I saw how some of my Portuguese–American friends were treated and didn't want to be considered different. During these years I totally dedicated myself to a change that, through my teenage eyes, would possibly take me into a realm of true Americanism. I didn't want to speak the language of my parents, and my first language. I didn't want to attend Portuguese–American functions. I didn't want to associate with people of my cultural background. And I felt ashamed of my Portuguese connections. I didn't want my parents to speak to me in Portuguese, although they didn't speak another language. And because society insisted on mainstreaming, I felt that to be Portuguese was to be incomplete or imperfect. Much as Amy Tan explains in her engaging essay "Mother Tongue:"

> When I was growing up my mother's 'limited' English limited my perception of her. I was ashamed of her English. I believed that her English reflected the quality of what she had to say. That is, because she expressed them imperfectly her thoughts were imperfect. And I had plenty of empirical evidence to support me: the fact that people in department stores, at banks, and at restaurants did not take her seriously, did not give her good service, pretended not to understand her, or even acted as if they did not hear her. (Tan, 136)

This feeling of imperfection, of awkwardness, implemented through an alienation process where the main, so–called white, Anglo–Saxon Protestant beliefs are above all else, instigated within my most recondite inner feelings the thought that, to be different was to be less, inferior, undesired. During one's teens, when one wants to be accepted by one's peers, being from a different cultural background can be a painful experience. Our "melting pot", and its forceful homogenous idiosyncrasies, alienates the immigrant's image. This process of total miscegenation permeates a segregation of thoughts and ideas. Although one may live next to the Anglo–Saxon majority, we were segregated through such realities as: lack of language; different social and religious practices; and a sense of a lower, totally misunderstood socio–economic class. As a teenager, I wanted to desperately be totally American. To me, this was only achievable by renouncing my Portuguese heritage, culture, language and even family. As Ilan Stavans mentioned in his book *The Hispanic Condition*:

> Is the American dream accessible only when one denies one's own past? Once again, the young people are pushed to the margins, their journey from the barrio to the classroom is marked by depression. What's wrong is a lack of genuine interest by the institutions themselves. This country's Eurocentrism excludes Spain and Portugal as pillars of Western civilization... (Stavans, 183)

Throughout the next few years, into my early adulthood, mine was an existence of ambiguities and misinterpretations. I felt that in the American world, even though my sense of direction was totally embarked in that perspective, I was an outsider. Even though I spoke the language, used blue jeans, and frequented the same social institutions, I remained, within my most intimate feelings, an outsider. In the Portuguese–American community, I felt that the archaism of rituals and customs didn't play a significant role in the new world. And I was constantly reminded of such thoughts by society at large. As Stavans eloquently affirms: "To become full U.S. citizens, we need more than a passport; we need to reinvent ourselves, to rewrite our history, to reformulate the paths of our imagination" (Stavans, 190). It is this reinvention that as my adulthood progressed, I had to do. It was this process that permitted a new look at my unique existence between two different spheres. Without it, I would be lost in a world of alienation and frustration. But this transformation also has its costs. Again, Stavans states:

> This metamorphosis includes many losses, of course, for all of us, from alien citizens to full–status citizens: the loss of language; the loss of identity; the loss of self–esteem; and, more important, the loss of tradition. Some are left in route, whereas others forget the flavor of home. But less is more, and confusion is being turned into enlightenment. In this nation of imagination and plenty, where newcomers are welcome to reinvent their past, loss quickly becomes an asset. (Stavans, 18)

It is this invitation for a successful life in the total American status that promotes one to leave behind all the other idiosyncrasies. The losses that come within the theory of the "melting pot" are forms of estrangement that leave the immigrants on top of a bridge without knowing to which side he, or she, really belongs. And most importantly, this alienation tells you, categorically, that you must not belong to the two worlds. It is a constant reminder that one is a foreigner. To assimilate is to break off from the mother land, language and culture. To become truly American is to lose your ethnic tradition. If one chooses such a road then one becomes integrally confused with one's status. And there isn't a harsher feeling than not belonging to any society. The Asian–American writer Amy Tan masterfully displays and explores these ambiguities in her extraordinary novel *The Joy Luck Club:*

> I think about our two faces. I think about my intentions. Which one is American? Which one is Chinese? Which on is better? If you show one, you must always sacrifice the other. It is like what happened when I went back to China last year, after I had not been there for almost forty years. I had taken off my fancy jewelry. I did not wear loud colors. I spoke their language. I used their money. But still, they knew. They knew my face wasn't one hundred percent Chinese. They still charged me high foreign prices. (Tan, 304)

The subculture I am now comfortable living with is a direct result of many years filled with disconcerts and challenges. It was only through the world of education and literature that I learned to outgrow the humility I once felt from being Portuguese–American. The humility imposed upon me, and others, as a form of alienation, starting with having parents who, in the eyes of the mainstream, were different, and thus, less than. From having to hide my linguistic heritage with a prepared and artificial accent that made my words sound funny in English and phony in Portuguese. From having to lie about being born in the United States for I didn't want to be considered anti–American. It was the world of education and literature that liberated my fears of living on the hyphen. Through this transmutation I not only rediscovered my roots, my language, my history, my culture, myself, but also learned to cope with alienation in a different light. I began to feel part of an American system that must be multicultural, forever embracing all cultures and ethnic groups. My Portuguese heritage wasn't a hindrance and I began to proudly display my differences. Through education, and the world of literature, both in English and in Portuguese, I felt rejuvenated and reborn. I felt a new sense of self–esteem and worth.

Living on the hyphen has given me the ability to embrace the two worlds that compose my cosmos. Taking the alienation and turning it into a process of self–discovery has allowed a new respect for my past and for the historical past of all other ethnic groups. By living life on the hyphen, and breaking with the dogmatic principles of the "melting pot", I was able to acquire a better understanding of the contrarieties that comprise our two worlds. Today, I feel much more American and much more Portuguese. It is possible to live two cultures and two languages. If life on the hyphen, politically speaking, means living on the periphery, then I choose to always be on the purlieus of the American society.

Yes, *meus queridos*, these are simple, humble thoughts of what it is like to be part of two worlds. The journey can be arduous, but also very stimulating. Whatever road you choose to travel through, never let alienation put you in an ambivalent state. Let it be a decisive tool in guiding you into the multiple labyrinths that shall continue to compose, and enrich, the American experience.

Works Cited

Handlin, Oscar. *The Uprooted.* Boston: Little Brown and Company, 1951.

Stavans, Ilan. *The Hispanic Condition: Reflections on Culture and Identity in American.* New York: HarperCollins, 1995.

Tan, Amy. *The Joy Luck Club.* New York: Ivy Books, 1989.

MARINA CARREIRA

Marina Carreira is a Luso-American writer from the Ironbound area of Newark, NJ. She holds a BA in English from Montclair State University and a MFA in Creative Writing from Rutgers University. Marina works in higher education and is also a correspondent for the *Luso-Americano* newspaper. She is curator and co-host of "Brick City Speaks", a monthly reading series at Hell's Kitchen Lounge in Newark, NJ. Her work is featured or forthcoming in *The Acentos Review, Writing Disorder, Naugatuck River Review, Writers of the Portuguese Diaspora: An Anthology,* and *Paterson Literary Review.*

Shrinking Violet

On nights when the moon is a busker,
my granddaughter asks me again
about the sugar sacks me and my seven siblings
would suck on before sleep. Blue scraps
of fabric filled with sweet grains and tied
with carpet strings, a primitive pacifier
placed in our mouths to pass us into
the land of dreams. Oh dreams!
What are dreams but circus clowns
while we sleep?

We dip yesterday's bread in olive oil,
feast on goat cheese and drink wine
mixed with Seven–Up. My mind
wanders off to days before my parents
had pruned skin, our home more
than the rocky bones of a building.
I tell her stories of São Mamede:

early morning olive–picking;
face–washing in the pig trough by the well.
Father watching, adoring, alongside
dirt paths cleared by a mule's long days.
Stubborn goats and restless sheep;
stubborn restless sleepless
nights on potato sack–covered hay.

She listens in earnest, picks a scab
that's formed a comma on her knee.
Some tales are pink–powdered elephants,
some stories are old, ancestral bones.
On afternoons when the sun is a shrinking violet
it's her job, I tell her,
to know the difference.

Luso–American Ephemera in Avó's Old Armoire

Page from a Portuguese passport,
>   stamped one–way: 1973, USA.

Old coins
>   the color of a lizard's tongue.

Tassle
>   from the lip of my grandfather's Sunday loafer.

Ace of spades
>   curled at the corners, reeking of Winston cigarettes.

Polaroid—
>   my father's youth league soccer team.

My baby
>   tooth charm, dangling off a broken bracelet.

Christmas card,
>   the blue of "Boas Festas" fading.

NJ Transit ticket stub,
>   BROAD STREET stop.

Funeral prayer card
>   for Alberto Silva, village baker.

Flyer,
>   Amália at Carnegie Hall.

Penny candy
>   wrappers, crinkled, smelling of coat pocket.

Postcard of Nazaré,
>   a fisherman's wife in seven skirts, *with love, Tia.*

Gold medal of St. Antonio:
>   restorer of lost objects, never brought back

anything worth saving.

A Girl's Fado

Se eu soubesse que morrendo
Tu me havias de chorar
Por uma lagrima tua
Que alegria
Me deixaria matar
"Lagrima," Amalia Rodrigues

I learned sadness like a hunger felt in the middle of the night
watching my grandmother turn the pages of her Bible.

It wasn't a real hunger like the kind she suffered as a child–
a plate barely filled with cabbage and beans on a good day–

but an ache she sat with every morning till past noon, this lament
no one's hands could grasp, no one's shoulder could bury.

My grief wasn't illiteracy or remorse, but a shade as deep–
a knowing but un–having. A blue so black my heart purpled

on the playground watching wind move leaves, an ant carry
an acorn, a swinging girl smiling over her father's shoulders.

I learned how to cry watching Mother love my father:
redden the face first, bellow out till lungs almost collapse,

then let the body shake then slack until it's so damp all moisture
funnels out eyes first. Last, the deep sigh, like Earth groaning

at winter's first show. Some nights, my sadness released
when she'd lay, asking *WhyGodwhydidImarrythisman?*

A slow stream of lava over her cheeks, neck, a river of red
down the bed. I swore we'd drown side–by–side unless

Our Lady's pity was taken upon us: a poor dandelion dried up
too soon, another still yellow but on the brink of airborne bones.

Ironbound
Newark, NJ

Years before the bouquet of my palm dried,
the east side skulled my dreams.
These railroad tracks were my bones.

*

My hands grew fat as dahlias,
waiting for the train that never came.
Blood thinned with Riverbank water

darker than a murder of crows.
I made the orange concrete fortress in the park
my lungs, each breath carefully guarded

against sirens wailing like newborns.
Like vultures, neighbors swarmed
Portuguese bakeries and barbecues

after church, exchanged morsels of gossip
as peasants did cheese. My bastardized tongue
up and down Ferry St. Feet dragged,

heavy as sickly livers, past Five Corners
stores covered in *Special!* signs.
Eyes dropped, flattened soccer balls,

when older girls walked their breasts
down the street, perfuming the air
with *Heaven Scent* and mother's shame.

Men hid violin–stringed smiles
in the bar where my father left me
sitting on the red stool until night fell

on my neck, until I became
the plastic plant no one dusted.
Still, the extraordinary existed

when Avó's pigeons flew out after breakfast,
the gasoline–rainbow of their wings
over Ironbound like a promise from God.

Years before the bouquet of my palm dried,
this east side skulled my dreams;
these railroad tracks were my bones.

MILLICENT BORGES ACCARDI

Millicent Borges Accardi, a Portuguese–American writer, is the author of three poetry books: *Injuring Eternity, Woman on a Shaky Bridge*, and *Only More So* (forthcom. Accardi is the recipient of fellowships from the National Endowment for the arts (NEA), CantoMundo, the California Arts Council, Fundação Luso–Americana (FLAD), Barbara Deming Foundation, and Formby Special Collections at Texas Tech. *Injuring Eternity* received honorable mention at the International Latino Book Awards in 2012. Her recent work can be found in *Verdad; Babalonia; InterDISCIPLINARY Journal of Portuguese Diaspora Studies; Mantis: A Journal of Poetry, Criticism & Translation*, and the anthology, *Gavea–Brown Book of Portuguese–American Poetry*.

Breaking with the Old

(italics loosely based on Urban Dictionary entry under New Bedford)

Breaking with the old, it was a grand adventure
to end all adventures. Leave Aunt Mary and Uncle John
and the *city on the south coast where you can eat linguiça*
and Jag. A place *where you know to stay away from*
The Front after dark, where you *head down to the Fort*,
to light up or make out, *knowing that the Guatemalans*
all live in a van, you know that Sassaquin Pizzao
isn't really New Beige, but then you get dressed up
to go to the Madeira feast, or the Holy Ghost.
And even you *can prove the Dartmouth*
refs get paid off, you know that boys do play volleyball,
or they head to Puzzles if they're gay, market off to Strand if
underage, and troop to Bar 908 if they are forever
resilient. *Our* Portuguese *fishing fleet is almost gone,*
and everyone knows at least three people who deal.
You leave back for *cruising on the Ave*
until 2 on a Friday, leave back where you are,
hitting up the 24 hour Dunky's, doing a turnaround at Brooks,
leave back where you are,
a*nd maybe laugh at the imports in the Wendy's parking lot,*
laugh at the wall, the great wall of New Bedford
Mass, I say *aka 20 aka the secret city aka the new war zone*
Aka the new Bagdad aka the druggy capital of the world,
Aka my drama city where the humidity
makes me throw up on Acushnet.
AKA the Standard Times. *Aka a violent city*
aka a kaput city a dead city, this city wrapped around itself,
in a zone of deadness inside a blind spot,
of lacking, where there is *a lot of underground talent,*
and no one wants to get caught in the after dark, tied down,
or led back to what they call "A New," or "the New,"
aka new beige. And here's the bit most people don't know
this but *it's called the secret city because there is no snitching*
in New Bedford. No one ever tells. New Beige, a place where half

of the hell of this city don't even speak.

If I Had Not Read the Book, I'd Still Have Believed

Hanging there in white, a bride
of dried veil blossoms, alit
like an electrical
storm, a brutal spark or a stir spoon
of cream in gentle water but dry,
florescent, flushing, pale, solvent.
Solvent as a daughter vouchsafe, with
names like chamomile, hibiscus, hawthorn
devil's claw, lavender, night shade, honey
root, sarsaparilla, horseradish, myrrh.
My fingers are disappearing, now,
dissipating to powder. It was mortar and pestle,
a cold and fixed time in history.
Pagans. The Black Plague. Salem.
One sip of me could poison or
heal, tangoing down your backbone spine,
cold or dry or steaming, steeped
into a shade or overshadow of fresh tea,
brewed like a promise. Tea, drink in, stir
fast. This is not easy, lover, come to me
while whole. Come to me when I am
what is wanted, while effervescent, while
I am, while the mother stirs
on her axis, while there is a promise for
things. While there is still.
While the air is still.

Musings in January

I decided that it is not his body
although that perhaps
could have or used to have been
a reason and he is still pretty
but after watching a definitely B
chick flick in a hotel room
last weekend, it would suffice
to say that it is not, definitely not
the bull dog neck, which I also happen
to favor. Or the flat boxer's nose.
No, it is how in this hopeless movie,
and every previous film or still photograph,
or candid shot, he has made or posed for,
he looks at his women as if they
were a platter at a banquet, or ice
at an oasis, and he is an island surrounded
by water or a lake or he is a sailor.
And now he is lost, thirsty and lost.
So lost as if he wanted nothing more
than to drink in what all women in the universe
have to say
Even when he is starving, thirsty, dying,
Even then.
He would rather listen.

Arriving at the Place of the Pain

Arriving at the place
of the pain, there is street traffic,
and the moon is an ability
to float or fly above water or
the intensity of this why
and why not or how deliverance
from a year of crying happens.
It's been ten now and still
the human race is a different
location. The first death
of childhood, a neighbor
posed on her side, under a sheet,
her body rolled down
the aisle of St Luke's on Termino.
On a weekday, she was Marion.
On the Saturday, she was white,
her life painted on in weekly sections,
the trim, the careful patches
under the eaves. The old paint
showing through. Her Pall Malls
in the cigarette case purse.
Her husband, boasting a stubbly beard,
his skin showing thru red blotches.
We found him sitting in the first row.
Arriving at the place
Of the pain, weeks later,
my mother and I surprised Mr Ed,
in his nakedness, pushing
the apartment door open we saw him
chasing a figure, a pink nightgown.
We'd been bringing by kale soup,
in a glass jar secured with a rubber band.
Arriving at the place
of the pain I hold it at arm's length,
away from sensation, into the deep.

Start Here

It was like trusting
a stranger and letting
him into your house,
when you had a nagging
feeling he would turn
up later with a key.

Even as you answered
the door, saying
in an unfrightened
way, that you wanted
to be, were wanting
to be charitable,

There were thoughts
of a gang of men.
of him, just like this,
breaking
into your life,
throwing boxes,
looking for quick

answers, then
leaving behind
empty cartons.

Even when you tried
to put charity
first, you pictured
the unlocking
and a gun

You saw your
grandmother,
someone
asking for her
purse, then more.
Lots more.

SARAH CHAVES

Sarah Chaves is a first-generation Portuguese-American writer who attempts to tackle the confusion and the incredible distance that lies between the hyphen separating Portuguese and American. Since she began writing, excerpts from her working memoir have been published in The Emerson Review, The Notebook, and other journals. She was the 2012 recipient of the Scholarship for North American Writers of Luso Descent, a travel writers' workshop in Lisbon, Portugal. This year, she will be returning to Lisbon, Portugal and the Azores as a 2015-2016 Fulbright Scholar.

Dobra Lingua

I am not a master of the Portuguese language. I cannot hold a lengthy conversation in Portuguese without the stutter of a difficult word or falling back into the comfort of English.

I am the daughter of two Portuguese immigrants. And by that definition, I am not Portuguese but American. I grew up speaking and understanding both languages. But over the course of my twenty–two years my Portuguese has weakened and my English strengthened—twelve years of grade school and college, groups of friends who knew only English, TV and the media, and the increasing use of English in the house as the prominent language. Portuguese then became the language I connected back to my childhood. Up until a couple of years ago when I decided to stop fearing it—I would speak and write Portuguese no matter how many mistakes I made.

But just as I begin to believe I can reach a level of Portuguese fluency, I suddenly become hyper aware of just how deficient my English can be at times. I was lying on my couch a few weeks ago watching television when one of my favorite movies was about to begin, an early 1990's Halloween classic. I yelled for my boyfriend who was downstairs, "Hurry David, *Hocus Pocus* is giving. It's going to give right now!" David rushed up the stairs as I shouted again, "Close the light, hurry!" David then stood by the light switch but didn't flick it off like I'd asked. His confusion was perhaps one of the few times I encountered someone who didn't understand what I had said— the English I grew up with and used all my life was suddenly incoherent and unrecognizable. What I had meant to say was, "*Hocus Pocus* is about to play on television" and "Turn off the light"—what I had said instead was the most direct translation of those same phrases in Portuguese, *Hocus Pocus esta dar nu televisão, dar* meaning to give, and *fechar a luz, fechar* meaning to close— but even as I processed David's confusion in my mind, my tongue and mouth felt the unnaturalness of the correction as I told David that the movie wasn't giving but playing and if he could please turn off the light instead of closing it.

But these instances, these conversations lost in translation, have always been the clashing point, the place where my English and Portuguese fuse. Every time I curse under my breath and my mother overhears me she will say this: *Dobra lingua!* I then will open my mouth so it's clear to see inside, then dramatically fold my tongue over itself. My mother never appreciates the joke. I am always overly literal when she says this, directly translating her scolding into an action. I literally fold my tongue, as I do every time she tells me to watch my language, and revel in the way I can manipulate language.

So it should be no surprise when I say most of my family elders slip in and out between languages when speaking, seamlessly weaving intricate threads of English and Portuguese around each other into coherent sentences. I understand now, as with the scene with David and other encounters with non–Portuguese speakers, close friends especially, that this swirling in and out of languages is difficult to follow or to even comprehend without an understanding of both languages being spoken. However, the way my father spoke, before his voice was cut short, made as much sense to me as a sentence needing a subject and a verb. Here's an example of something he would say when he came home from work:

"Hello Sarita how're you? How's the schoo'? You *faze o* study real good—no Sarita. *O Papai não quer brinca*, no play righ' now, he too tire'. Papai's gon' eat firs'. He so hungry, been *sentado em* traffic ove' two 'ours! No *comida nu* van *para comer*. So *agora*, Papai gon' sit down, and eat wha' mommy made fo' food. *Ja comeste? Ja fizeste o teu* homework? Good. Tha's a good girl. Sarita, *faze um favor por Papai* and *da–me um* napkin. T'ank you princessa. Now *vai para dentro* and watch *o* TV. Papai *ja vem*. I'll be righ' there."

But please do not be so brash as to judge my father based on this example conversation or assume that he was an unintelligent man. He managed to remodel our entire house on his own, knew the dimensions of a room just by looking at it, could find his way around any city without getting lost, could make toys for my brothers and I to play with out of wood and plumber pipes—all the kinds of things I can't begin to imagine how he began acquiring them into his tool box. Yet most people who didn't know my father, like old friends and ex boyfriends, found him unapproachable. They found him the most ominous when he didn't speak at all. This fact hurts me now, as if they thought my father was a brute and nothing more. But that assumption is so far from the truth. Perhaps, and I'm saddened to think so, my father hid behind his tongue, letting his appearance exude strength and power, while his English speaking skills quivered in the corners of his mouth. I regret not addressing the issue then, pushing my father past his insecurities, and proudly proclaiming that there is no shame in his language.

Soon after my father died, my father's brother came to live with me and my mother and two younger brothers in America. Like my father did when he first arrived in this country, my uncle struggled with English. He still struggles. After a weary four years, he still cannot properly pronounce the word "year," always silencing the "y" and saying "ear." My youngest brother cracks jokes at him all the time saying, "Tio Marino you should come to high school with me and finally learn how to speak English the right way," and then lets the jab hang in the air. My uncle usually laughs it off, but as soon as my brother leaves the room my uncle's face suddenly changes, as if wondering if maybe he should.

It is no secret, though my uncle tries his hardest to hide it, that my tio Marino fears his language limitations. He is scared. So often when we ask him why he doesn't do things by himself he replies by saying that he's "scare'." Again, he lets his response come off as a joke but there is undeniable true fear behind his words. And why shouldn't he be scared when there are so many language barriers in front of him: employees at our local grocery store, bank, and coffee shop that do not understand him, do not know that when he says "friskis" he means "Friskies," do not know that he doesn't know how to fill out a withdrawal or deposit slip for his own bank account, do not know that a "media *café*" means a "medium coffee," and do not know that his intelligence exceeds that of his language limitations.

I am often caught in the middle of such conflict. My uncle hates talking on the phone with someone who doesn't speak Portuguese, oftentimes simply passing the phone to me with an exasperated look on his face and his hands in the air in frustration. By handing the phone to me, he can simply quit the conversation and let me fix the problem or figure out the reason for the call. But the one thing my uncle hates more than talking in English on the phone is dealing with people face to face. When my uncle got laid off from work and had to file for unemployment, he had to go to the local office to file some paperwork. Within a half hour he was back home storming through the front door and said, "Those piece a shits don' understan' me."

I sat at the kitchen table doing some homework when he put a blue piece of paper in front of me and said, "Sarita, *assina* this *papel* for me. They say I did wrong, They no give me my *dinheiro*."

I put my homework aside and looked down at all the empty textboxes that hadn't been filled out except the ones asking for an address and signature. "Okay, you need to fill out the information concerning your job. You need to write in these boxes the reason for your lay off and for how long you'll be expecting to collect, stuff like that."

Clearly daunted by the task at hand my uncle said, "*Podes fazer por mim*, please?" He asked if I could do it for him, fill in all the boxes, as he continued, "If I do, those idiots gon' make me go home. Maybe you come wit' me, they see you, they give me the money." I assured my uncle that I would help him fill out the form, but I wouldn't go to the office with him, because I wanted him, just him, Marino Chaves, to do this for himself and realize that he could do this on his own.

We had a very similar conversation recently, a situation that involved my very own job. We were out of bottled water, so I sent my uncle to my Walgreens with my employee discount card. When my uncle returned, he put the water down, handed me my employee discount card, and the receipt. "They no take the *cartão*," he said, telling me how they refused to give him the employee discount. He said they didn't believe him when he told them he was my uncle who lived with me, and that they accused him of probably finding my card outside on the floor somewhere and stealing it. My uncle tried to explain that he had moved from the Azores to live with us but his English only got worse when he got nervous. He didn't understand their objections so he left. He paid full price for the water. I immediately got in my car and went to Walgreens, furious, and asked to speak with my manager on duty—without a minute's wait—to which he then profusely apologized for the whole situation, explaining how he found my uncle oddly suspicious, and how he found it hard to believe that such a non–English speaking man could be related to such a well–spoken girl like me.

Perhaps it's situations like these and witnessing similar experiences of my father's that drove me towards language rather than away from it. I thirsted for new words and enjoyed using them properly. I reveled in the way I correctly said "thirteen" instead of my father's "tirteen." I knew my ABC's when I was two, got 100% on all of my spelling and vocabulary tests, and did consistently well on written essays. I blew through one journal after the next, constantly writing, always putting my thoughts down on paper as if the act itself would make my ideas permanent. I thought about my father's experiences often, and never, in all my life, did I want to experience the same hardships with language, did I want to not be easily understood, and to have the inability of communicating my thoughts and needs to other people. Perhaps it's this fear of being unable that empowered me, but cast my father and uncle in the foreign shadows of America.

This is my guilt. My father remained in the shadows all his life; I never did my part to get him out. Whereas, in my uncle's case at least, I still have time to get him out, to walk him into the sunlight. I can help him put his fears aside and allow him the chance to absorb English rather than cower in front of it, such as working on pronouncing the "th" sound, instead of inserting a "ta" or "de" sound. A great accomplishment for him would be to, without faltering, say "Thank you" instead of "T'ank you," pronouncing the name of his employer properly, and correctly asking "Where's Sarah?" instead of "Who's Sarah?" The day he is mindful of such corrections, and doesn't laugh or make a joke of it, is the day he may finally realize his own potential. He may finally believe in his own autonomy.

The way I think about my uncle's English, and the way I think about my father's, is that it is imperfect, not broken—after all, how can any language be broken as if it is a roof with a leak? For something to be broken, is for that same thing to be damaged, injured: a broken mirror, a broken leg, a broken contract, a broken spirit. But language never felt like it was something as tangible as a chair or as abstract as a promise to be capable of breaking. So to then say my uncle's English needs to be fixed, is to advise something I do not agree with, "I can' believe!"—so that I would say instead my uncle's English can be improved, worked on, but never fixed. Just because I am well-spoken doesn't mean I believe my English to be perfect, because I still make mistakes: is my English then the same level of "brokenness" as my uncle's? I believe I will do my best to improve my uncle's English, but for my sake and his, I will not make his tongue forget the imperfections, forget the rolling Portuguese "R," forget the "O" motion of his mouth with the "ão" sound, but simply make room for all the equally beautiful sounds of the English language, too.

EMANUEL MELO

Emanuel Melo was born on the island of São Miguel in the Azores and immigrated to Canada at the age of nine. His articles and short stories have appeared in *Cleaver, Mundo Açoriano, TWAS (Toronto World Arts Scene)*, and on the website of the Canadian Centre for Azorean Research and Studies. His short story, "Avó Lives Alone," was a finalist in the Writers' Union of Canada 20th Annual Short Prose Competition for Developing Writers in 2013 and was published in *Memória: An Anthology of Portuguese Canadian Writers*. He is currently working on a collection of short stories that draws from his Luso-Canadian heritage. He lives in Toronto.

The Cottage Visit

The drive to the cottage was just over three hours. By the time Melissa picked up her father-in-law at the nursing home and got on the highway she knew that they would not get there much before noon. Her children, Chelsea and Austin, sat in the back of the SUV. They read their Harry Potter books in silence while Melissa tried to engage the old man in conversation. This was hard to do as of late. He began to lose his memory a year back and found himself with little he wanted to say; that's when his son decided that Francisco was a possible danger to himself and could not continue to live alone. The nursing home was pleasant enough and he had a room with a view of Christie Pits. He did not get out much anymore so today's outing was a rare treat.

Melissa asked him about life in the nursing home, she talked about the kids, told him how Chelsea was going to grade six next September and Austin into grade five. "They are both getting glasses next week," she said. Francisco smiled. Although his grandchildren did not speak Portuguese they had been taught to greet him with the Portuguese word for grandfather, *avô*. Melissa called him *pai*. She wasn't even Portuguese, but she liked to call him by the endearment of *pai*, father, nonetheless. The old man turned around to look at his grandchildren sitting in the back, engrossed in their reading. He smiled at them. He didn't say much lately and Melissa wasn't sure if he understood all that she said. But she still talked to him as if he did, knowing that he would much prefer to hear what she had to say in his mother tongue, a language that, since his wife died, he only heard in his mind.

By the time they arrived at the cottage by the lake, everyone else had arrived. There were the usual greetings of hellos, how have you been, we haven't seen you for a long time, hugs, and introduction to new visitors to the cottage. "This is Clair," said Lindsay, the hostess for the day, "she's thirteen and staying with us for the week." Chelsea and Austin were close enough in age and the adults knew that they would get along. There was also a French girl, Madeline, almost fourteen, visiting for the summer from a small village near Lille in the north of France.

"Bonjour," said Chelsea, trying to impress Madeline with her limited knowledge of French. Lindsay's grandchildren, Connor, nine, and Lily, five, were shyly looking on.

Francisco stood still in the confusion of introductions until Lindsay came up to give him a warm hug. "It's so good to see you." They had not seen each other since his wife died two years ago. Lindsay, Melissa's old aunt, had also been recently widowed and her eyes, looking into Francisco's, conspired to betray the truth of how painful it was to be alone these days. "I can't stay alone at the cottage anymore," she confided in him during a quiet moment while the children swam before lunch.

The lake water was warm and soothing and the kids played Marco Polo in the water. "Marco!" called out the girl who was "it," swimming with her eyes closed, hoping to touch someone to win the game. "Polo!" yelled everyone else to help the swimmer find them. After a long swim in the sun, Lindsay called everyone back up to the cottage for lunch. There was the usual cottage fair: burgers and hot dogs and buns in plastic bags, mustard and relish and coleslaw and potato salad. While sitting at the table, Clair read her book for a few minutes and a picture taken at Disney World fell out of her book. Austin saw it and picked it up.

"You've been to Disney World?"

"Yeah, just this past June," Clair confirmed.

"Oh, my God, we love Disney World. Chelsea, she's been to Disney World! She's so lucky."

Chelsea and Austin jumped with delight at finding someone who, like them, had had the Disney experience. They missed Disney World. For the past five years they had gone every summer to Disney World but not this summer.

The children sat around the deck table under the shade of an umbrella. Madeline was having a hard time following the animated conversation in English between the others and retreated into the privacy of her MP3 player. Lily jumped into the conversation to say that she, too, was going to Disney World in August. She listened intently to the conversation between the older children. Connor, the only other boy in the crowd, and the oldest, stayed alone inside the cottage, playing his video games. Francisco sat at the table with everyone else. He was content to eat his hamburger in silence.

"Did you go on Thunder Mountain?" asked Chelsea.

"Yes." Clair nodded.

"Splash Mountain, too?" Austin wondered.

"Yes."

"Tower of Terror? I love Tower of Terror!" Chelsea said.

To all the rides in the Magic Kingdom, Hollywood Studios, Animal Kingdom, Epcot, Clair confirmed that she had gone on them.

"Did you eat at Chef Mickey's? How about Liberty Tree? And how about the Princess's Castle?" Chelsea and Austin were eager to know as much as possible about what Clair had seen and done.

"Did your family drive there?" inquired Chelsea. Yes, they had, Clair confirmed with a nod, her mouth full of burger.

"We drove down last year, too." Austin said.

Francisco ate his hamburger silently. He found it comforting to hear the children's chatter and was content to be here rather than sitting alone in his room all day or in the lounge room where only the staff came by every so often to say hello. He did not see his grandchildren often. He did not see anybody too often anymore. Today was a treat. But he had no reference for what they talked about. When he raised Paulo, his only son, born in Toronto, there had been annual summer trips to Niagara Falls and Centre Island but it was mostly Sunday visits to family and friends. That was the way the Portuguese families spent their Sunday afternoons, sharing their traditional foods from back home, prepared with ingredients bought in the Portuguese grocery stores of Kensington Market. They would sit around the kitchen table, reminiscing about their lives of long ago on the island of São Miguel in the Azores, eating *bacalhau* and *pasteis de nata*.

These days, everyone he knew of his generation was dead and his nephews and nieces lived far apart from each other, some in Woodbridge, another in

226

Forrest Hill, and yet another in faraway Montreal; none of them stayed in downtown Toronto where their families first started out in the 1960's. The past, so remote now that at times it felt to him as if it had never happened at all. But he still had his son and his daughter-in-law and they both made a special effort to say a few words of Portuguese when they visited. His grandchildren, however, could not master their ancestors' language given how infrequently they heard it spoken.

After lunch, everyone headed back to the water for more glorious swimming and another game of Marco Polo. Melissa sat on the deck, sheltered from the unforgiving sun. The children were slathered in sunscreen. Lindsay sat in the shade under the trees, her old fair skin also keeping her out of the sun's rays. Francisco sat in a folding chair by himself on the deck looking out into the lake water, watching the children's heads bob up and down, causing ripples in the warm blue water. He had almost drifted into sleep when he heard Melissa cry out *"Ai, Jesus!"* pronounced something like zezuz. Melissa had heard her mother-in-law say that phrase often enough and she had found it amusing if not endearing, and repeated it in moments of surprise or panic when one of her children fell down or got into trouble.

At hearing the old familiar exclamation, something his wife used to say all the time as a reaction to all things that surprised or startled her, Francisco perked up as the words connected him to his past and it brought back memories of those days when he and his wife were together. He missed not being able to think about the past anymore. His life seemed like a dream to him lately, as if it never happened, until those words, familiar and familial tapped his mind and for a few seconds the Portuguese sounds of *"Ai, Jesus"* jolted his former world back to the present. Those two words, spoken in Portuguese, woke his dormant memory of the past and for a moment he could almost smell the scent of the Atlantic Ocean rising up from the lake water below. He smiled.

Soon the beautiful day came to a close and Melissa was eager to leave before rush hour started. She gathered their belongings, said goodbyes to everyone; said how much they enjoyed the visit. Chelsea and Clair promised to text each other over the holidays. Lindsay invited them all back again for next summer and hoped that she could see Francisco more often. "You call me," she said giving him a hug and he nodded smiling, knowing that he would never call. He hated the telephone and had nothing to say, anyway.

On the trip back into the city, Francisco slept most of the way, lulled by the heat trapped in the car windows and the tiredness from the day spent outdoors. He found himself awake only much later, alone, already in his room, sitting in his lounge chair, surrounded by photographs hanging on the walls, assuring him that he had lived those moments and known those people smiling at him in faded black and white. There was one of him with his wife; they were both smiling, sitting on a bench under an old tree in Furnas, on one of those excursions they would take out into the countryside on Sunday afternoons before they were married and oh so happy and young and still unaware that one day they would leave their island home to the so far away big world of Canada, where they came to live and end their days, and where Francisco could remember it all again just now, after a visit to the Muskoka lake of that afternoon.

NANCY VIEIRA COUTO

Nancy Vieira Couto's poems have been published in numerous magazines and anthologies, including *The Iowa Review; Mississippi Review; Prairie Schooner; The Southern Review; Good Poems, American Places; The Gávea–Brown Book of Portuguese–American Poetry;* and *Poetry Daily: 366 Poems from the World's Most Popular Poetry Website*. She is the author of a full–length poetry collection, *The Face in the Water*, which won the 1989 Agnes Lynch Starrett Prize from the University of Pittsburgh Press, as well as a chapbook, *Carlisle & the Common Accident*, published in 2011 by FootHills Publishing. Her awards include two National Endowment for the Arts Fellowships, a Creative and Performing Artists and Writers Fellowship from the American Antiquarian Society, and a Constance Saltonstall Foundation for the Arts Grant. She was born in New Bedford, Massachusetts, received a B.S. in Ed. from Bridgewater State College, and earned an M.F.A. in English from Cornell University. During a varied career, she has worked as a teacher, a temporary typist, an insurance claims examiner, an executive secretary at a TV station, and a subsidiary rights manager at a university press. She now lives in Ithaca, New York, where she is completing a manuscript of poems based on historical characters and serving as poetry editor of *Epoch*.

Angie Appropriates a Bar or Two[13]

of "Dixie," belts them out over dinner
dishes, muffs the lyrics, hums the rest,
ad–libbing the refrain. All she knows
about the land of cotton is it's far
away and for all she cares can stay there.
She's done with cotton, never wants to see
another spooling frame or harness. Done
with drop wires, heddles, and that sonofabitch
of a boss with the permanent leer
rusted across his face. Still, it wasn't
all bad, she thinks, reaching for
the Brillo and remembering how Eddie's
tough–guy voice and cocky defiance
attracted her attention toward his hazel
eyes and wavy hair parted straight
down the middle. But mostly
she threaded her own heddles, went home
to ma and pa, emptied out her pay
envelope on the claw–footed table,
the tiny clump of bills, Liberty standing,

Liberty walking away, walking uptown
on Saturdays, browsing in the aisles
of the 5 & 10, stopping to play "I Love
Coffee, I Love Tea" on a toy
piano, when who should appear
but Eddie and—what's this?—he wants to walk
her home. Barely five feet tall,
she's smart and high–principled. He's tired
of his floozies with their come–ons and off–
color jokes, ready to settle down
with a nice girl. Any nice girl. Even
this one, whose big, apprehensive heart

---

[13] First published in *Gettysburg Review*, Volume 7, Number 4 (Autumn 1994). It also appears in my chapbook *Carlisle & The Common Accident* (FootHills Publishing, 2011).

clatters inside her ribs. So they talked
about the mill, about his five brothers
and four sisters, mostly about how he
was going to make it someday, make it
big and, by the way, could he take her
out next Saturday and the Saturday after?
He'll have to ask her pa, she says and he,
not one to waste time, decides to get
the asking over once and for all.
Twenty minutes later they're engaged
to be married, her ma putting a pot
of coffee on to keep the patterned wallpaper
from spinning. Angie holds the doily
down with her elbows while her pa
rolls a cigarette. Even Eddie
needs something to hold on to as the textile
industry moves south, as Mussolini
moves on Ethiopia, as Hitler
moves on the world. The world survives

for now, and now here she is, a ma
herself with a sinkful of greasy
pots to scrub, a third–story tenement
to mop and polish. She launches into "God
Bless America," still marveling over
all the trouble music can get you into.

Grains of Salt

See the skinny boy with the puffed–up chest,
the one who will grow up to be my father
unless he drowns? The other boys jump
and paddle and scrabble up the fissured
rock and jump again. Golden boys,
they glisten in the sun. Their splashes of
laughter and palaver make it look
so easy. But my father knows the tides,
finds footholds on the rock's submerged flukes
and tail, and calculates how long
he's got before the waves roll in again.
He climbs the rock's rear slope and finds a space
among the other boys and cracks a joke
or two and suns himself and keeps an eye
always on the lapping of the water.
And when the tide turns, he pulls his shirt on
and leaves the way he came when no one's watching.
He is nine years old.

I know this story: One day an older boy,
fooled by my father's bluff and swagger,
shoves him in. My father hits the water
flailing, nothing underneath his feet
but water, and, when he opens his eyes, nothing
but blur, underwater soup, and sure
dissolution. He would have said a prayer
if he had been a praying boy. Instead
he tries to imitate the moves he's watched
the others make, their dogpaddles and kicks
and crawls, and somehow gets it right,
and he's swimming. He's swimming!

He liked to tell that story. And he swam
often that summer, sneaking off from chores,
until his mother, who also knew the tides

were rising, were ruffling over neighborhoods,
over families, over her own children
poised like a flight of steps in the center
of her heart's house, caught him sneaking back,
pulled him closer, bent, put her tongue
to his arm, and licked the telltale grains
of salt. That was the end of swimming
for my father,

           but not the end of salt.
She could taste it on her tongue, in her blood,
and she knew the tide was turning but could not
have known that soon she would be a widow,
that she would board the Canopic with her children,
one of them still a toddler and another,
the boy who would grow up to be my father,
a real handful. And after that expanse
of salt and water, she would be one of many
in a new land whose language she would never
master but whose history she would help
to flavor. She would never know that she
was the salt of the earth.

Madragana Wears Her New Name

Madragana wears her new name
tight under the chin and scrubbed of all
impure exotica: such a short
syllable, a stub, a stutter, and
it hobbles her. *Maior,* she has become,
or *Mor,* for short, a Christian name, all dots,
no dashes, all staccato. Her steps
are circumspect, tidy. She walks
a dotted line but won't sign anything.

A name should sashay across a room,
should swing its syllables and sway its consonants
and toss its vowels. A name should be a dance
out the door and over a dazzle of sand
in time to the phrases of the oud.

For your immortal soul, he said, standing
Godfather. He knows she knows she has
no immortal soul. Neither does he,
although he's a good man and a good king.
Bad husband, though, but not her husband, though.
His ear is to the ground, and the ground
rumbles. She knows he knows she knows
he's thinking of the children. But her new
name hangs stiff as penitential garb
under the Algarvian sun.

My Father Glows in the Dark[14]

mansions of memory, cruising secret
corridors, unlocking rooms. He has me

where he wants me, trapped on the living–
room couch pretending not to notice

the hole in the slipcover or the insistent
odor of urine. He repeats

himself, telling stories about people
I don't know, choosing not to hear

questions I hardly bother asking
across that distance. So I watch the new

worn spots in the wall–to–wall and mostly
tune him out. But here's one

I haven't heard before. My father rolls
his chair close enough to whisper

as if we're in cahoots. *She was the cook's
daughter. I said I'd bring her home*

by midnight. As he talks I see
greedy–eyed gulls, a flight of stone

steps to a garlanded pavilion,
the promise of the possible sloshing

in the tall, cool drinks, riding the waves
of hot music. Here he stops to wallow

---

[14] First published in *Salamander,* Volume 4, Number 1 (1996). It also appears in my chapbook *Carlisle & The Common Accident* (FootHills Publishing, 2011).

in my attention. I can almost see
her platform shoes. I can almost hear

her laughter, the way it bubbled over
the face of his watch. *We missed the last*

ferry. We had to spend the night
in the sane house. The sane house! I see

the madhouse upside down doing a last
wobble before filling in the blank

suddenly sunlit rooms with ruffles, teakettles
and bookcases. Then I see I heard

wrong, of course, and what he really said
was "seine house." He's back there now, lost

under nets and floats and ocean smells
and trouble in the morning. The story

is over. Thanks to miracles of cataract
surgery, his eyes are bright, the better

to see me. But he doesn't see me.
He just sits and stares out the back

window at the point where the road
gives up at the horizon.

The Unfinished Girls in Pink[15]
(A Meditation on Digital Imaging Technology)

marquisette clutch their bouquets
and tilt apart, shy of the bridal

axis. Eight and ten, they are
spinning, gussied, skirted, overskirted,

underskirted, hooped, ready to roll,
ruffled, wired bonnets set for all

the world like inverted tarts spilling
meringues of bow. Oh, how that banana—

curled girl I was ate up every cake
that spelled *forever!* Now they tell me photos

of my backyard alfresco wedding years
later can be digitized, repeopled

like a Renaissance masterpiece, Madonna
and Child positioned carefully among

saints and chosen members of the family
of so—and—so. *As usual she'd have*

nothing to wear. She'd spend the night
turning up a hem, jumbo pink

rollers gently logjammed on her head.
I think I'd let her slip in by the day

lilies, a teapot of a woman
poised forever steeping first flush

---

[15] First published in *The Bookpress Quarterly*, Volume 2, Number 2 (May 1997). It also appears in my chapbook *Carlisle & The Common Accident* (FootHills Publishing, 2011).

memories. Might as well, while I'm at it,
decolorize my pink–flowered lawn

wedding dress, wrap it in a cloud
of lace. Might as well make the cake

a corniced wonder, iced façade festooned
with swags and dotted with dragées

of expectation. Well, I expect
I'm finished now, photos put away

unchanged. Not to be changed. A mixed
bouquet is what it is, the past imperfect

as the present, where the dead are with us
differently. Hear them in their tissue–

lined boxes, the way they fret and rustle
and course for all the world like that

river no one steps away from.
After pictures, there were toasts and cake

and jordan almonds. Everyone held on
to someone as the world began to spin

off flowers and finger sandwiches and promises
not to be kept.

PAULA NEVES

PaulA Neves was born and raised in and around Newark, NJ's Ironbound section. Her writing has appeared in Pilgrimage Magazine, Gávea-Brown Journal, Luna Luna Magazine, Quiddity International Literary Journal and other publications. Her artwork is featured in the Glassbook Project collections Provisions, Changed Relationships After 9/11, and Domestic Violence. She is a Sundress Academy for the Arts fellow (2015), a Canto Mundo fellow (2014), and has received scholarships/residencies from the Luso-American Development Foundation, the Disquiet Literary Program and Westchester Poetry Conference. She performs with Kale Soup for the Soul, a Portuguese-American artists collective. For more information, visit paulaneves.net.

Train to Lisbon

We took a train down the Portuguese coast and got drunk,
on the wine and pastries we carefully packed in the trunk
we hoisted everywhere on our two–week Silver Coast junk–
et; the small bottles of *tinto* and the *pasteis* eased our post–argument funk.

We stopped sulking long enough to ease the wine and pastries from the
          trunk,
relieved, after missing the express and waiting for hours in a park in Cacém;
the small bottles of *red* and the *sweets* eased our post–argument funk
better than the stale bread we'd bought fresh in Sintra the previous day.

We waited sullenly for hours in that park in Cacém.
"That's not how it happened!" I hear you object
because we'd found Byron, not bread, in Sintra the previous day.
But lyrics aren't much concerned with the facts.

"That's not how it happened!" one always objects,
and sustenance is one of the fictions of our days.
Besides, lyrics aren't much concerned with the facts;
so this is what I mean put a different way:

Bread is just one of the fictions of that day,
as was that cumbersome love, I mean, trunk, and the sweet drunken talk.
So this is what I mean put a different way:
When the train got to Lisbon, I walked.

The (Almost) Married Couple's Guide to Tourist Traps

In Lamanai we learned how the Maya might have sacrificed their hearts
while we, lapsed vegetarians, ate local spiced sweetmeats ourselves

to read the future in splayed seagull carcasses along the Great Salt Lake
so that New Orleans Indians would last until the next apocalypse

in that Baja town where trannies pass for wives until the real thing comes
        along
while we, women ourselves, played possum for the Day of the Dead

so that west of Oranjestad you could swim with fishes in the Mouth of Hell
and I could watch you, with something halfway between envy and regret

until Oporto offered up a river of English wines—
so we could toast our never staying long enough in one place.

Three Season Year

In the summer,
he made barbeques,
the noxious billow of lighter fluid
meeting match flames
over splintered sidewalk branches,
turning Nixon's plans and Green Stamp circulars,
like everything, to ash.

He never bothered me with small talk,
never said, *"You too can grow up
to be President."*
He drank Pabst and muttered, *"Bullshit."*

In the autumn,
he disappeared down the storm cellar hatch
bearing a handful of arbor grapes,
and crates of those he bought,
and emerged ages later
with gallons of new wine.

I never needed an explanation
for why, like the wedding jugs at Cana,
they never seemed to run out.

In the winter,
when the weather had turned
chill enough that the acrid smoke
from the dripping chicken fat
was warm and comforting
(he still made barbeques to save on gas,
indifferent to the cold in his wifebeater and work pants),
he never said, *"Take this in to your mother."*

She never said, *"Take this out to your father."*

The following spring,
I hear he planted a kitchen garden.

11th Birthday

They are all here.
Neighbors, cousins, mother's co–workers,
primped in polyester on the plastic–covered couch,
their children with their hands on everything
(*badly educated* as Ma would say—
except on special occasions).

To impress them, on my 11th birthday
I sit at the piano, the one Ma bought,
after two months of Saturday shifts,
from Maria Marques, because her daughter, Diana,
after just one year of learning herself,
started giving lessons and outgrew it.

Va la, go on, play us something understandable,
they urge, instead of all this jangling.
Then tell your sticky–handed brats to leave, I think,
when Diana, already a lady at 12, takes her place
beside me on the bench, turns to the last page,
and starts the count, quieting them instantly.

Surprise! I clank through my own *Happy Birthday*.
Diana hums to keep the beat—futilely,
as everyone sings it in their keys.

How long this lasts I'll never remember.
Meanwhile,

the food waits on the table we never use:
Wonder Bread, Shop Rite cola,
yellow butter crème cake from Coutinho's
decorated in cursive thin as veins
(from which those little fingersmiths
have already swiped the day).

Apart from this there are the staples:
potatoes, rice, the deep fried cod fritters
they all call *balls*, which, if I look
at Diana now, would make me titter—
understanding, as I am,
how concerned they all are with *appearances*.

So, instead, I hit a wrong F sharp on purpose
and offer it to Diana (whose conducting never wavers)
as small revenge for playing along with our mothers,
who wouldn't want us to misrepresent
why at other people's houses we get the stare of death
if we dare to entertain a *yes*
when we are offered
anything.

Capricornucopia (or The Dream of the Goats)

Goats appeared at the door,
asking to eat the house from inside out.
It was Christmas, so we let them enter.
The drink–laden guests parted.

Sure footed on the walnut–inlaid parquet,
the beasts made for the manger first,
ate the fake hay with unbridled relish.

The billygoat then eyed the end tables
my girlfriends and I had saved from curbs
and I had carried on my back
to whatever places we were calling home.

All the females followed billyboy's suit—
whatever they're called—girlygoats?
I know what they are but regardless

everyone looked at me as if the goats
could see through walls—
an insight out of Freud or Focault.
My new girlfriend looked pissed.

The goats made for the sofa.
"What are these girls called?" My girlfriend insisted.
Stuffing fell about us like snow.

The billygoat toppled the tree.
Blown glass ornaments blew everywhere.
Some shattered. Some dangled
from his horns like disco earrings.

"Androgyny went out in the 80's,
when you were still young,"
I heard at my ear.

I hoped it was the voice of the devil
I didn't know—a future lover perhaps,
her flutes as piercing, her heart as cloven
as any Pan I could ask for (and have).

But it was only my mother,
who whispered, "Did you ever
turn on the oven?"
Then added, "You're starting to get whiskers,
just like them."
Tender, the words went through me like a horn.

Mercifully, someone shouted, "They're headed for the table!"
And so the goats were. Like midnight buffet tourists,
they charged the sweetmeats, the Mouton Cadet,
the *chanfana*[16]
 like grandma used to make.

"Cannibalism. At Christmas no less,"
a faceless relative
tsk tsk'ed.

Let them.
Let them be goats.
Let them eat everything—

                          even the bones.

---

[16] Traditional Portuguese goat or mutton dish wine-stewed in an oven..

Kiss My Black Ass: A Meditation

"Kiss my black ass!" he said. He said it after he got home from work. He went around the house saying it –in the garage while compulsively arranging his yard tools; in the bedroom as he shucked his blue Dickey's and flannels to don his other uniform, the baggy, torn jeans, guinea tee and flip flops that he wore at home year round, whether to mow the lawn in the summer or take out the garbage and shovel snow from the stoop in the winter. "Kiss my black ass!" He said it to anyone who would listen, or not, family or foe, the two indistinguishable to him, I supposed. But mostly he said it to himself, as he entered and moved around the kitchen fluidly, hypnotically, almost gracefully as he stooped in the pantry, hoisted the gallon of Gallo or his own homemade wine onto the kitchen table, pulled a long glass from the dish drainer, set it down purposefully, unscrewed the cheap top, tipped the gallon over the glass. By now, the imperative to kiss his black ass was a murmur, a barely audible buzz that filled the kitchen with the holiness of a sacrament and the unrelenting urgency of a mantra. It didn't matter if anyone was there to witness it—whether me, mildly disgusted but fascinated too as I paused in my rarefied trajectory to my room or a friend's house, or my brother, distracted enough from his GI Joe's, baseball cards, or borrowed *Hustler* to emerge for a soda. "Kiss my black ass!" my father might growl then and yank the Shoprite ginger ale from my brother's hands, to top off the ten ounces of wine already waiting in the glass with enough carbonation to pass as a spritzer, as if anyone would ask.

By his fourth or fifth "spritzer," my mother was usually home and beginning to boil or fry whatever it was she had asked me to take out to defrost that morning before I left for school. By then too, my father no longer moved with ascetic vigilance, but openly knocked around, slamming down the gallon and the glass still runny with the dregs of the last drink, sloshing the wine into the glass and spilling it, no longer bothering to pour enough soda in it to pass. "Kiss my black ass!" he shouted, grabbing my mother's ass as he passed her on his way to the sofa. She knew enough of herself and him by then to say nothing, having developed her own discipline, her own meditation as she went through the motions of cooking and getting my brother and me set before she left to take a bus downtown to Wilfred Beauty Academy, where she spent her evenings getting her hairdresser's license.

Years later, I'd tell friends, lovers, whoever was there that my father was often fond of saying, "Kiss my black ass!"

"Is your father black?" someone finally asked me.

In all those years, the obvious had never occurred to me.

"No," I responded, shocked. "It was a saying he picked up on the docks, from the black guys he worked with. He thought it was funny, I guess. So he repeated it over and over."

"Oh," was the usually only response, before we moved on to the next topic.

MIGUEL MONIZ

Miguel Moniz is from New England, born in an Azorean and Cape Verdean migrant strawberry farming community on Cape Cod, Massachusetts. He lives in Lisbon.

News from New Guinea

a Pliant Philippic

*

The thought in his head when she reached for his hand,
brown, worn, slipping to his waist in easy rest.
His arms too heavy to lay fully over her shoulders.

In the embrace he could still smell the waft
of was it bacon grease, cloy her kitchen
must have been yet from sometime last night.
Even like this she still had the need to clang about her stove.

It was always something else they talked about,
the leak under the eaves from the loose shingle leaving
dingy water marks in the crook of the ceiling,
how George was coming by to till the flower beds for
planting on Tuesday, you know they buried Mrs Andrade last week,
David's grandmother, and John Pacheco showed up just for the feed.

He smoothed her rough hair with one last press
and ambled down cellar to fix the shelf,
as he said, his reason for the visit.

He had to move three boxes of old newspapers, some going back to the
80s,
why she kept them all, he never knew never asked why,
just pushed them out of the way, cardboard in slide across the concrete,
reached to pull and place the cans on the floor and with
the heat of the light bulb dull at his shoulder, the hammer and nails,
put the shelf back in place and at least an hour was gone.

Walking up the stairs, the table was already set for the late lunch where he
ate and she
served, first a soup then a pork chop then his second glass of wine without
waiting for

him to ask.

They sell these velvet buttons, he said, winding his finger around the size
while holding the knife,
I saw them at work, over near home furnishings, you should get some for
that sweater,
I'll bring them next time I come by.

Things like that on this sweater?
You think I have time to be sewing buttons all day?

The bread soaked up the last color of red pimenta and garlic wine sauce off
the plate.

He pushed up off the table and nestled the broom to rest back in the corner
after sweeping,
kissing her forehead, his goodbyes, he walked out the door.

At the store, he thought, they must already be wondering to where I could
have gone off.

News from New Guinea

the Mariner's Maenad

*

She let it drop in a Botswana hut,
then it was dragged back to her goth–taffy village as it goes
children playing in circles
with their dead ancestors' bones,
and then it hopscotched to Moçambique
and it was perfect on the beach,

and in Mindelo it went mad and showed kind,
and then it beat in Baia, where it burned it burned,
then across it floated down these banks,
as it goes.

With the estuary gulls crowing their witness she said,
play your clarinet and I'll spin like its Tết
and every other race was a beautiful place
but what any one has quite this sun?

scene

Ruddle the wandering night
a concertina twist.
Pressed to the breast the organ
breathing through folds
exhaling inconceivable orients,
and in a key button brass flash
the light off the Tejo
was tricked for the babbling Menai,
wet wind blowing down from Yr Wyddfa.

Blow! Blow on a tide to the Mississippi Gulf,
rain storms and shiny golden trumpets will lead us on our way.

JOZHE

Jozhe Fonseca is a media artist, who has worked with script, motion and everything in between. Jozhe began as an illustrator with a Bachelor Degree from F.I.T., moved forward to multimedia design and animation from the Open University, completed post-graduation studies in Art Education at Kean University, cartoon illustration at IADE, New Media at Nova University, and a Lighting Design Professional Master's at NYSID. Jozhe has participated in the European project Media, involved in the production of an interactive TV program in the fiction and entertainment genre with the development of two original scripts. Jozhe writes monographs in the subject of communication and has a Master in Communication Arts from NYIT. In the Portuguese Community he set–up and designed the online Luso Newspaper and their bookstore and the online site for the International RTP Contact television programme. He participated in exhibits promoted by the Consul and by the East Ward Council Member. Awards: Xingshi–Cup 2013 nomination with a Luminaire Design. People's Choice Award Green Kids Game Art NYS Business Plan Competition. Winner Google Maps Portugal with Manuelino Gothic. Open University Best Interactive project. Interactive TV, E.U. MEDIA Program Project publication at Lusofona University Publications. Honorable Mention Alcantara Festival, Urban Project National Palace. Photography award Avante children theme. Jozhe is affiliated with IESNY. DLFNY. Collegiate Entrepreneurs Organization Club U.S.A. CG Educational Material Source Reviewers dl.acm.org, Bit Film Club. Portuguese Club of Arts and Ideas.

Que curiosidade reveladora
subitamente conquistadora
que nobre fim para se empenhar
o desejo de a conquistar,
a face que desabrocha gloriosa
algo dominadora e orgulhosa.
Para o conseguir nada o segura
se para tal partisse a nervura
não iria nunca parecer
de má morte padecer.

A certain sniffing curiosity
conquers him so suddenly
a noble goal to strive for
a desire to measure against her
blossoming face full of self esteem
somewhat proud and domineering
to the aim nothing held him back
if he were to break his neck
it would not have seemed
a bad death to him.
(Trans.)

A tua beleza contemplo
a tua face em assombro
combina esta admiração
o respeito e a veneração

A pele, etérea beleza espelhada
lembra cerâmica vidrada
os teus lábios escarlate
ofício de um homem de arte

E quando da Primavera for indício
sucedendo ao Inverno num vestígio
contigo de novo quero estar
o sal nos teus lábios saborear.

At your beauty I gaze
awe inspiring is your face
wonder mingled with
veneration and respect.

Your skin of a pale Celadon glaze
Traces of an antique ceramic vase
your lips sang–de–boeuf
an artful man´s craft.

And when the haze of spring
is following winter´s trace
I want to be with you again
a taste of salt upon your lips.
(Trans.)

MANUEL CARVALHO

Manuel Carvalho nasceu em Cicouro, Miranda do Douro, em 1946. Colares e a Batalha fora lugares que o viram crescer. Viveu grande parte da juventude nos Outeiros da Gândara dos Olivais, nos arredores de Leiria. Fez a guerra colonial em Angola. Depos correu muitas terras (Porto, Paris, Lisboa, etc.) até chegar a Montreal, no Canadá, em 1980. Exerce a profissão de designer industrial. Iniciou–se nas letras em Leiria, no semanário "A Voz do Domingo (Suplemento literário "Arrancada"). Em 1979, alcançou o 2° Prémio num concurso de contos do Diário Popular de Lisboa. Organizou os Jogos Florais Luso–Canadianos (1983,1985). Tem colaboração espalhada por diversos jornais e revistas do Canadá, França, Estados Unidos e Portugal. É autor dos livros "Saga" (1989), "Um poeta no paraíso" (1994), "Parc du Portugal" (1997) , "À beira–Main" (2003). "Rostos, Olhares e Memória" (2012), "Rostos, Olhares e Identidade" (2013), "O homem que falava com as flores" (2015). Em 2012, publicou vários livros em formato e–book: "Ti Vida", "O homem que falava com as flores", "As belas manhãs de Maria Constança", "Entre Morros e Capim". É coordenador da revista virtual "Satúrnia – Letras e Estudos Luso–Canadianos.

Montesinhos

Este ano, lá para o meio de curtas férias em Portugal, encontrava–me com a família em Miranda do Douro e como tivéssemos a intenção de nos deslocar a Braga, para festejar o S. João num banho de multidões, decidimos ignorar as novas e tentadoras vias rápidas e aventurar–nos pelo acidentado e montanhoso percurso via Bragança–Chaves.

Trajecto sem dúvida mais demorado mas que, em contra–partida, proporciona ao viajante o regalo de paisagens e panorâmicas deslumbrantes que talvez só quem habitualmente está ausente sabe apreciar de olhos abertos e usufruir em plenitude.

Por volta do meio–dia, já em pleno parque natural de Montesinho, detivemo–nos para saborear o farnel bem mirandês à sombra de frondoso castanheiro.

Estava um dia quente mas aprazível, do fundo da ravina chegava–nos o cantarolar duma ribeira de águas cristalinas e debruçados sobre a sinuosa estrada, braçados de florezitas brancas, parecidas com malmequeres, heroicamente agarradas às fragas e ao chão pobre, saudavam–nos gentilmente.

—E se levássemos algumas para o Canadá?—alvitrou a minha mulher, de alma amolecida pela beleza envolvente.

Dito e feito. Arrancámos alguns pés que, com mil cuidados, acomodámos num saco de plástico, juntamente com alguma terra humedecida que os sustentasse na longa viagem que os esperava.

Desconhecendo o seu nome de baptismo, acordámos chamar–lhes montesinhos, em homenagem à terra que as viu nascer. Palavra com musicalidade que quanto mais vezes a pronunciávamos mais nos agradava, o que era de bom augúrio pois todos nós sabemos como é importante recomeçar vida no estrangeiro armado dum nome que caia nas boas graças gerais.

À chegada a casa, aqui em Montreal, mesmo antes de desfazer as malas, o meu primeiro cuidado foi ir plantar os meus montesinhos no quintal.

E, não obstante a aparente fragilidade, ou não sejam eles rijos transmontanos, resistiram corajosamente à transplantação e, mal passada uma semana, já começam a arrebitar as orelhas, espevitados pelos novos ares e pelo húmus gordo.

Por vezes, sinto–me um pouco constrangido por os ter arrancado à sua liberdade selvagem e os ter aprisionado na prisão dourada do jardim mas se tiverem uma alma, como acredito que a têm todos os seres vivos, estou certo que compreenderão, tal como os leitores, as minhas pungentes e profundas razões. Para me redimir, prometo que se os montesinhos tiverem garra para resistir ao rigor do próximo inverno e proliferarem vigorosamente na primavera, irei utilizar todo o poder de persuasão ao meu alcance para convencer a vizinhança a adoptá–los e acolhê–los, por sua vez, nos seus jardins.

Se tudo correr bem e nenhum inesperado cataclismo ecológico vier impedir a sua natural proliferação, é muito possível que, perdida a memória da sua origem, daqui a algumas gerações, algum desprevenido turista luso–canadiano, de viagem a Portugal à procura das suas raízes, em pleno parque natural de Montesinho, exclame admirado:

—Olha, aqui também há montesinhos, aquela flor canadiana!

E eu, se essa história da vida eterna não for uma patranha, do lugar onde estiver, não poderei reter uma gargalhada, mais uma vez divertido e surpreendido com o fascinante e sempre remoçado espectáculo da vida.

Tributo

Encontro–o, vezes sem conta, ali no parque, sentado num dos bancos que bordejam o lago povoado de patos selvagens.

Nunca lhe soube o nome, nunca quis saber em que localidade portuguesa nasceu. Para mim, é o emigrante desconhecido e isso me basta.

Esta definição tão sumária assenta como uma luva à sua figura rústica, robusta, talhada na telúrica pedra das serranias portuguesas.

Pela rugas profundas, como sulcos de arado, do rosto, pelas mãos nodosas e possantes, pelo olhar de aço, é fácil adivinhar um homem tenaz, coriáceo, habituado aos trabalhos pesados e ao rigor de climas inóspitos.

«Andei muitos anos na construção, trabalhei no estádio olímpico, estive nas barragens da baía James, aquilo é que era frio de rachar.»

As palavras não deixam transparecer qualquer queixume ou ressentimento. Antes pelo contrário, reflectem o orgulho do homem que nunca baixou a cabeça perante as contrariedades da vida e que tudo soube aceitar estoicamente, de dentes cerrados e coração largo.

Geralmente, é ao entardecer que os nossos passos se cruzam. Eu gosto de olhar o voo caprichoso da meia dúzia de andorinhas, lá no alto, incansáveis na perseguição às nuvens de mosquitos. Ele adora ouvir o trinar dos melros refugiados na folhagem dos carvalhos.

«Na minha terra corre um regato, no meio de muito arvoredo, onde é um regalo ouvir cantar os rouxinóis. Mas olhe que aqui os melros também não cantam mal, não me farto de os ouvir.»

Entre nós, os silêncios são longos e eloquentes. Mas também há dias em que os pensamentos anseiam voar mais soltos, precisam de se transformar em palavras numa alquimia demorada, sem pressas.

«Hoje passei o dia a tratar do quintal. Já tenho aquilo para ali cheio de tomateiros e alfaces. Este ano também semeei umas leiras de feijão de trepar que um vizinho me deu, vamos lá ver o que aquilo dá. Amanhã, talvez plante uns pés de couve. Os *quebécois* chamam–lhe couve portuguesa mas na minha terra sempre lhe ouvi chamar couve galega." Após tão longo e inabitual discurso, fica a observar a aspereza das mãos castigadas. «Agora que já não trabalho, ajuda–me a passar o tempo.»

Disse–me que morava perto do parque mas já me esqueci do nome da rua. Deve ser num daqueles duplexes que para ali há, com umas hortas nas traseiras que são um mimo. Só mesmo obra dos italianos ou portugueses amorosos da vida, que por lá andam a semear mão–cheias de poesia.

«Na minha terra trabalhei nos campos desde criança, ainda não esqueci o que aprendi. Qualquer dia, passe por lá para eu lhe mostrar a minha obra. Aproveitamos para beber um copo do meu *vinho*, este ano saiu–me de estalo. Usei pela primeira vez uvas chilenas e não me dei mal.»

Quando está mais predisposto para a conversa, fala–me da casa que mandou construir na aldeia natal, do bom pedaço de terra que tem ao redor, onde plantou um magnífico pomar.

«Plantei lá muitas árvores mas as de que mais gosto são as cerejeiras. Quando lá chego no verão, estão sempre carregadinhas de cerejas encarnadas que é um encanto. O meu irmão é que me trata daquilo, caso contrário estaria tudo ao abandono, a criar urzes para os lobos. Eu e a minha mulher fartamo–nos de trabalhar nas férias, nem sei para quê. Os meus filhos nunca lá vão, não querem saber daquilo para nada. Mesmo que não lho confesse, às vezes acho que têm razão, há sítios mais descansados onde ir passar as férias. Já têm outra forma de ver o mundo, não lhes posso levar a mal.»

É desnecessário perguntar–lhe se está arrependido de ter emigrado. Basta ler–lhe a determinação do olhar para antecipar a óbvia resposta.

«Quando eu vim para cá, Portugal era uma miséria, morríamos de fome. Aqui fui bem recebido, a vida foi por vezes difícil, mas tudo se passou, o trabalho nunca me meteu medo. Hoje tenho quase oitenta anos, a saúde não me falta, criei os filhos que, graças a Deus, têm bons empregos, os netos gostam de mim. Quando as saudades apertam, meto–me num avião e vou até à terra. O que mais posso pedir?»

Há dias em que lhe dá prazer rememorar os primeiros tempo da chegada, quando tudo era desconhecido, nas raias do irreal.

«Não tinha cá ninguém e não percebia patavina das línguas do país. Tenho muito a agradecer a alguns portugueses que já viviam no Bairro Português, se não me tivessem amparado, não sei o que teria sido de mim. Quer saber qual foi o meu primeiro emprego? Nem lhe passa pela cabeça.»

Solta uma gargalhada, inesperada em homem tão circunspecto, que até sobressaltou os patos no lago.

«Fui apanhador de minhocas, veja lá! Íamos ao anoitecer, em grupo, para os campos de golfe, com uma lanterna na testa e uma lata atada à perna, e era um apanhar nelas que só visto. Quando conto isto em Portugal, nem acreditam, pensam que é cantiga minha.» Divertido, passa a manápula pelo rosto, acama os cabelos grisalhos mas ainda bastos. «Depois já foi melhor, os meus amigos arranjaram–me trabalho numa padaria de italianos, a amassar pão, tudo o que vinha à rede era peixe.»

Ontem, apareceu acompanhado pela mulher. Franzina, azougada, tagarela, um pouco mais nova do que ele, veio, rapidamente, espalhar umas pinceladas mais vivas nas nossas conversas tantas vezes insípidas.

«Este malandro, mal acaba de jantar, sai logo porta fora. Desconfio que anda para aí a arrastar a asa a alguma rapariga." Dá uma palmada amigável no joelho do marido que sorri, meio encavacado. De pescoço esticado, varre o parque com os olhos inquietos para logo se voltar para mim, pronta para desatar o saco num chorrilho de palavras que se atropelam umas às outras, apressadas por voar em bando.

«O meu marido já lhe deve ter contado a vida dele mas olhe que a minha também não foi fácil, principalmente no princípio. Trabalhava numa fábrica de casacos, a ganhar à peça. Aquilo era todo o santo dia agarrada à máquina, quantos mais forros pregasse mais ganhava, era trabalho de escrava. Costuma–se diz que Deus escreve direito por linhas tortas, é bem verdade. Quando a fábrica fechou fiquei toda aflita mas, passado pouco tempo, encontrei trabalho, nas limpezas em casa de uma senhora judia, foi como se me tivesse saído a sorte grande. Ela gostou tanto de mim que, passados poucos meses, já era eu que tratava de tudo, fiquei a ser a governanta da casa e já tinha outra portuguesa para me ajudar nos trabalhos mais pesados.»

Calou–se, com as mãos cruzadas sobre o peito, para ganhar fôlego. Oportunidade que o marido aproveitou para se desculpar, com um olhar penalisado:

«O senhor deu–lhe trela, agora tem de a ouvir. Esta mulher quando começa a falar não há quem a cale.»

«Lá vai por ti, passas dias seguidos quase sem me dar uma palavra, às vezes parece que lhe meteram uma rolha na boca. O senhor quer ouvir mais esta...»

Na calmaria da tarde, ela continuou o seu tagarelar sem fim, eu fiquei a seguir o voo das andorinhas, o marido de ouvido à escuta do canto dos melros que até pareciam que se esmeravam só para lhe dar prazer.

Sei que aquelas criaturas que aqui estão sentadas ao meu lado, naquele pacato anonimato, nunca estarão debaixo das luzes na ribalta, nunca verão o seu nome escarrapachado nos jornais, morrerão como viveram, fundidos na natureza, com a naturalidade das árvores que cumpriram o seu ciclo, entre muitas, na floresta.

Contudo, quando por vezes me imagino talentoso escultor capaz de talhar uma estátua de homenagem aos emigrantes desconhecidos, é aquele rosto lavrado a formão e aquelas mãos rudes do homem e, frente a frente com ele, o rosto afilado, fremente, vivo, atravessado por coragem inabalável, da mulher, companheira das boas e das más horas, que gostaria de ter engenho para perpetuar no calor da pedra ou da madeira.

CATARINA COSTA LARANJEIRA

Catarina Costa Laranjeira was born in Lisbon, Portugal to a psychologist mother from the Azorean island of Faial and a diplomat father from Lisbon. She has spent many years living abroad in Mozambique, South Africa, Hong Kong, Portugal, Canada and the United States. She received a bachelor of science in economics from the University of Victoria and works as a research assistant doing public health research in pediatric primary care at Boston Medical Center—the city's largest safety net hospital. She is also on the executive committee for the Portuguese–American Post–graduate Society.

Life Lessons from an Orange Tree

My iced coffee is in a large, clear plastic cup. It tastes burnt and bitter—a poor oasis in the humid Northeastern summer. A band of marching children sings folk songs, carrying a red and green flag that belongs to another paradise—the kind assumed to be my home. Similar in size to California, with a third of the population and a more convoluted history, Portugal is the place of my birth. But ask any nomad where home is and they will point to tribesmen with a gentle shrug and contented smile. For now, the Bostonian heat would do until the next destination.

My surname, Laranjeira, has an unusual meaning behind it. Laranjeira is Portuguese for orange tree. Its roots are in Sephardic Judaism, the religion of my grandmother. And in honor of that tradition, she planted one in our country house outside of Lisbon. As years passed, my father's career took us to many lands: Mozambique, South Africa, the United States and Canada. I quickly fell in love with the nomadic lifestyle. But no matter where we went, I would gravitate towards this tree. Why was it so important? The answer would not be clear for nearly two decades.

Born under the Salazar regime, my grandmother was placed into an orphanage by parents that could not feed her. A smart and resourceful woman, she quickly adapted to the hardships that faced her, and thrived. She taught herself fluent French and how to read and write during an era of rampant adult illiteracy. Meanwhile, in the archipelago of the Azores, other relatives had sons called to fight a war they opposed. Tired of living under fear, and inspired by constant contact with adventurous foreigners, they escaped through an expanding telecommunications company as engineers across three different continents. My father carried on the tradition of hard work and adaptation through international travel.

During those twenty years, we ventured into the Land of Oz. My earliest memories are in war—torn Mozambique inside of our Beira compound. A six—foot tall fence and armed, nameless guards encircled it and us children lived oblivious to politics. Race, ethnicity and nationality had no meaning—only the kindness of other adults and children. One was the child of our neighbor's cook. Everyday we found companionship through a two—inch

270

wide hole in the fence. No matter how much mother protested, I snuck out every afternoon to exchange stories, chewing gum and jokes. There, crouching inside green bush I found solace as the bodies piled higher on the streets. Eventually, we left behind this land and moved back to civilization where guns, starving children and hushed tones exited daily routines.

Through my father's occupation we interacted with several Portuguese communities. Our language was the same, but our common experience was not. Many had formed before I was born, from an era that faced different challenges, had different concerns and experienced different political realities. But nobody spoke about the new realities, and how quickly Portugal was and still is changing in a globalized world. It wasn't long before I gave up having a Portuguese identity and embraced life as a third culture kid–belonging fully to no culture, and partially to all. Adaptation turned my siblings and I into cultural chameleons, navigating social situations with the objective to blend in. My grandmother passed away and the orange tree was cut down, as much in real life as in memory.

Back in Boston, I watch the annual flag raising ceremony hosted by the Boston Portuguese Festival in front of City Hall. Gathered around me are new faces of Massachusetts's second largest ethnic group–my friends, the young scientists and engineers that hemorrhaged out of Portuguese academia into foreign lands. There was no political persecution, or politics driving them–simply the desire to pursue interests and passions in laboratories or industries that could accommodate them. We are the new generation, the university educated that chose paths less travelled by.

As we sing the national anthem of my supposed home, that orange tree comes to life. They may not be third culture kids, but my friends understand that success happens by shedding habits that prevent it. Perhaps we are not so different. Change is impossible if you live in the past, but it occurs to me that–like the communities my father served–remembering is important to guiding adaptation.

I finish my iced coffee from Starbucks and throw it away, smiling. Years of ignoring her *laranjeira* gives me an important revelation: Without the past, change is meaningless and the fruit not as sweet. I join in on the singing, feeling like a true nomad. I have discovered my tribe.

ROSE SILVA KING

Rose Silva King was born in Modesto, California, in 1944. Her parents were both from São Jorge. Her father was a farmer and dairyman. Her mother is a homemaker. Rose grew up and attended schools in Modesto. Between her junior and senior high school years, she spent six weeks in Guatemala as a student under the auspices of the American Field Service organization. She has traveled extensively in Guatemala. She has taken part in an archaeological dig in Belize and in a sociological study of the Maya in Yaxunah, Mexico. She has traveled to Italy, Germany, France, Austria, England, Spain and Portugal. She has visited the Azores many times, especially São Jorge where she still has many relatives. She received her B.A. in Spanish literature from Dominican College, San Rafael, California, and her M.A. in Spanish literature from California State University, Sacramento. She returned to Modesto and married Michael King, her high school sweetheart. They have been married forty years and continue to reside in Modesto. She has been, among other things, a travel agent, a teacher, a nun, an interpreter, a stepmother, a real estate appraiser, a homemaker and now an author. Her novel, *A Cow for the Holy Spirit (The Journey of an Immigrant, the Azores to California)*, was published in conjunction with Portuguese Heritage Publications of California and is in its second edition. Subsequently, she had it translated into Portuguese under the title *Uma Promessa ao Divino Espírito Santo (A experiença de um açor–americano)*.

Longing for my Homeland

Ever–pulling homeland
My heart and soul yearn for you
Pátria, place of my fathers
Land of cliffs and sheltered coves
Flashing waterfalls and greening hills
Rocky paths trod by generations

Land of farmers and of oxen adorned with gold–tipped horns
Of cows, mottled black and white, wary and gentle
Giving milk to make round, thick cheeses, tangy when aged
To be eaten with coarse cornbread, freshly baked
Removed with flat–handled spatulas
From ovens ember–warmed with sapling branches

Island of earth and sea and sky and God
Of thick–soled shoes and black–shawled widows
Of rites that make each season valued on its own
Without TV cameras or reality shows
A cycle reflecting nature and the Church
Easter, Pentecost, wine–making, sausage–stuffing

Smoky kitchens, wooden floors, storage cellars
Newborn chicks, motley colored, trailing
Mother hens who scratch to find treasured corn kernels
Children with rosy cheeks, caramel–colored hair
Unprimped, braided.
Cow–licked boys with shy smiles

I long for your goodness, your earthiness
For your poverty of material and your wealth of spirit

SAM PEREIRA

Sam Pereira received his BA from California State University, Fresno, where his teachers included former U.S. Poet Laureate Philip Levine, Peter Everwine, and C.G. Hanzlicek. He also earned his teaching credential there one year later. From Fresno, he traveled to Iowa City, where he wrote, taught, and lived for two years as a member of the Iowa Writers' Workshop. He received his MFA from the University of Iowa and went on to two decades of unrelated work in agri–business. He currently teaches English in California's San Joaquin Valley. Mr. Pereira's books include: *The Marriage of the Portuguese* (L'Epervier Press, 1978), *Brittle Water* (Abattoir Editions/Penumbra Press, 1987), *A Café in Boca* (Tebot Bach, 2007), *The Marriage of the Portuguese— Expanded Edition* (Tagus Press, 2012), *Dusting on Sunday* (Tebot Bach, 2012), and the recently released*Bad Angels* (Nine Mile Press, 2015). Along with the above, he has been anthologized often, including in *The Gavea–Brown Book of Portuguese–American Poetry* (Gavea–Brown Publications, 2012) and the very well received and respected *The Body Electric—America's Best Poetry from the American Poetry Review* (W.W. Norton, 2000). His poetry has been included in magazines as diverse as *The American Poetry Review*, *Antioch Review*, *Blackbird*, *Manoa*, *Poetry*, *Poetry International*, and*Prairie Schooner*.

In the Name of the Holy Ghost
—for Susan

In the afterglow of the event,
She wrestled joy. The Portuguese
Were praying for her,
In their not so subtle ways:
Hail Mary, this is Susan,
And even though she's Jewish,
We like her. We understand
That she's married to one of us,
A poet. A lost soul, until
Her. So we dance. Soon,
We will enjoy *sopas* together.
She will always be his, but
As of right now, she belongs
With us, as well. Hail Mary,
You were a Jew, too, yes?
We all agree: Pereira
Has every reason to continue
Calling himself a poet,
So long as our new friend
Lets him kiss her in the name
Of everything right in the sky.

Sonnet Declaring the Wind Victorious

There has always been wind.
The kind that hits you in the face,
And screams, "I'm back. You
Remember me. The one
Who insists that you squint,
Presumably to show how fierce
You continue to be, but really,
I mean really. Isn't it
About protecting yourself
From the armaments of sand
I've been throwing your way
All these years?" You just can't
Harbor this wind for much longer.
Your pockmarks want to smile.

Salvation of Any Kind

It was in January, during a year
When the fog came early,
Trying to cover up our crimes.
I remember her, delving
Into the photographs captured
During our escape into Lisbon.
It had been the only time,
When faced with despair, we turned
At the corner with the broken sidewalk,
Looked up at the church
That was staring back at us,
And decided to laugh. Just laugh.
We didn't drop dead then,
Or now, as the guilt
Rolled off our shoulders
And into the gutters of Lisbon.
The Jew and the altar boy
Had come to grips, kissing each other
Under the Portuguese moon.
The fog continued to cover us,
And in Heaven, if there was such a place,
The owner nodded, ordering
More jazz! More jazz, in the names
Of those who came dressed in fog
Every year, about this time, to
Protest salvation in unholy Lisboa,
Or anywhere else that seemed real.

The Suck of Love

There is little left now:
Oysters hide in the bay,
Praying, as only oysters can,
For the stunning dark waters
And the clouds of sea dust
To hide them in peace.

On the water's edge,
An oblivion of restaurants:
Glasses clink because
It's someone's birthday,
Or a young boy and girl
Just got laid for real
And they are thinking:

How real, how painless,
What a great lie our parents
Told us all these years.
The oysters want them
To continue their numbness,
Eat their salads, look
Gleefully into the turquoise

Of their contact lenses,
And go home to jump
Into bed. The oysters
Just want to be oysters,
Without glasses and without
The young waiter who
Would serve them up

With a smile for anyone
Glancing into each
Other's moist eyes with love.

Scars and T–Birds

This one is about scars.
Those that stay hidden
Next to your liver,
Building nerve and strength
To break out in the middle
Of the night and leave
You bleeding. They would
Never think of taking off
Without signing their names
In your blood; leaving
The signatures resting
On your belly, wet
And candy apple red,
Like the '56 T–Bird
You once promised yourself
That you'd drive down
An abandoned and nameless
Northern California beach.
Scars and T–Birds. Neither,
It seems, meant to fly.

DARRELL KASTIN

Darrell Kastin is an American writer, born in Los Angeles, California, in 1957. His father's ancestors came from Belarus, at the start of the 20th century. His mother was born in the Azores, Portugal, and is the daughter of Azorean poets and journalists, Francisco and Josefina do Canto e Castro, who left the islands at the end of World War II. He is a novelist, short–story writer, poet, musician and composer, solely devoted to his art, and much influenced by Azorean and Portuguese music, history and culture. His short–fiction has appeared in *The Seattle Review*, *The Crescent Review*, *The Blue Mesa Review*, *The Windsor Review*, *Confrontation*, *Gávea–Brown* and elsewhere. In Portugal he has work in NEO Magazine and Oficina de Poesia. His first novel, *The Undiscovered Island*, was published in 2009 by Tagus Press. Currently out of print, it won the 2010 Independent Publishers IPPY Silver Prize in Multicultural Fiction. His short–story collection, inspired by the myths and people of the islands, *The Conjurer & Other Azorean Tales*, was released in December 2012.

The Secret Place

> *So for centuries the peak has stood, sublime and quiet,*
> *but even now, its crown is warm; there, unexpected at that*
> *altitude, there are warmth loving species of butterflies.*
> —Bernard Venables, *Baleia! Baleia! Whale Hunters of the Azores*

Emilio Borges disembarked at the wharf in Madalena and walked stiffly to the bus, struggling to hide the pain that made him move with such difficulty. He carried a bag filled with a change of clothing and other belongings, from which a butterfly net protruded.

He sniffed the air appreciatively as he walked away from the boat.

Ah, it is good to be back on Pico once again.

Emilio stepped onto the waiting bus. He nodded at the driver and sat down, then took out his handkerchief and wiped the sweat from his forehead. He ignored the driver and the others on the bus who turned to look, perhaps curious as to why he, an old man, was carrying a butterfly net.

Emilio glanced out the window toward Pico, but the mountain was covered with clouds. He thanked God that his first venture off the island was finally over. It would be his last, no matter what anyone said. He was sure of that. He'd had enough of doctors. And boats. Though he had lived his whole life on an island, he was a man of the land, of the mountain that was Pico, not of the ocean.

The bus quickly filled, then started the half–hour trip to Santo António, winding along the narrow road which circuited the island. He stared out the window, refusing to look at the other passengers, though he had seen one or two neighbors board the bus. He looked out at the green fields and the dense foliage of the checkerboard gardens, closed off by black walls of volcanic rock—walls that hid what lay inside, the way his body had hidden the disease for so long.

I won't sit helpless and wait for death. Doctors would rather have you crawl into a grave and be finished with it.

The bus dropped Emilio off in nearby Santa Luzia. He continued on foot down the road toward his home in the neighboring village of Santo António. Two of the villagers, Maria Inês and Isabel Fagundes, had scurried off the bus before him. They stood gathering their parcels and bags.

"Poor man," they said, shaking their heads, watching their silent neighbor make his way, step by painful step, toward his home.

The women waved when he looked at them.

Too weak to wave back, you old busybodies.

"What does he have in that bag, I wonder?" Isabel Fagundes said.

"He looks like a ghost," Maria Inês said, then moved her lips in a silent prayer, as she crossed herself.

"As if he can't see or hear us," Isabel said.

"Poor Maria Alice."

Emilio managed to smile at the thought of two women who couldn't possibly understand what he was doing with a butterfly net. He kept looking over toward Pico to see if the summit had broken through its shroud, but observed that it was still hiding its face.

"Only two days separate us," he said to the mountain. "Then, we will be together, eh? You, me, and the butterflies."

At last Emilio reached his home. He took out his kerchief and wiped the sweat from his forehead, then carefully folded the kerchief again and put it back in his pocket. His every breath came with a struggle. He waited a moment before entering the house.

Maria Alice had her hands full. She had soup on the stove and a dish of *bacalhau* on the table. Manuel was still out in the fields; he had grown into a fine, strong man. Antónia helped her mother with the meal. Antónia's child,

Dionísio, had recently been born, and Emilio was pleased to be a grandfather. Maria Alice nearly dropped the food when she saw her husband enter the house.

"Emilio! What are you doing here? Back so soon?" She rushed up to him, and peered at his face. "What is wrong? What happened?"

Maria had an uncanny ability to detect the truth, as well as a fine nose for deception. Emilio knew he couldn't lie to her, and knew that by looking at him she would suspect the worst. Maria didn't have to state with words that he looked terrible.

"What did the doctors say?" she asked.

He didn't answer. She had fought fiercely to go with him to Terceira, but he had refused, insisting she stay home—he had wanted to go alone. He put down the bag and went to the cupboard. He took down the bottle of *aguardente*, poured a glassful and gulped it down. He poured another glassful and sat at the table.

"Well?" Maria Alice said. "What did they tell you?"

"Nothing," he said finally. He knew he had to tell her now. He took a deep breath. "I am going to climb Pico. I decided on the boat back from Terceira."

"You are going to do what?"

He sat back as his wife stared at him in disbelief. He might as well have said that he was going to the moon. "I will climb Pico."

"I can't believe my ears," she said, raising her hands with her palms up, the way that had always made him smile. "Why? What about the doctors?"

"I'm through with all that. The cancer is everywhere, and I am an old man. There's nothing they can do."

"Maybe you should go to some other doctors," Maria Alice said, softening her voice to a more conciliatory and persuasive tone. "We could go to São Miguel, see a specialist. They will do something, no?"

"There is nothing the doctors can do now but quicken the work God has already started. No, I will not go to any specialists. I have only one wish and that is to climb the mountain."

Maria puffed herself up, the way she did when she was angry, and folded her arms over her chest.

"You've never climbed Pico in all your life," she said. "It makes no sense. Why should you do this? Why now?"

"Because I want to."

"Who will go with you to guide you?"

"No one. I must go alone."

"Dear God, save us! My poor husband has lost his mind. An old man, and he is going to go off on a crazy adventure and get himself killed!"

Emilio smiled, "She's worried about a dying man getting killed."

She ignored his comment, then noticed the butterfly net sticking out of Emilio's bag. "What is this?" she said.

"A net, to catch butterflies with," Emilio said.

"A what?"

"Listen woman," he said. "I met a man in Terceira, called himself a naturalist. He told me that at the top of Pico there are butterflies that can be found nowhere else. They live by the warmth of the crater. There and only there."

"So?"

"So, I want to see this butterfly."

The next day the whole village discussed the news that the dying man, Emilio, had lost his senses, and was going off to chase wild butterflies.

Emilio's oldest friend, Luís, who owned the café, tried to talk him out of his plan.

"There's nothing up there, old man," Luís said. "It's cold. Too high. Nothing grows up there, and nothing could live up there."

"How do you know?" Emilio asked. "Have you climbed up there to see? The naturalist told me that the warmth of the volcano keeps the butterflies alive."

"I don't need to go up there to know he was pulling your leg, Emilio. He's probably laughing right now, a good joke to tell an old man, yes?"

"It was no joke, Luís. The man had pictures. He showed me one he had caught, too. I am going up to see for myself."

Luís stared at his friend, a stubborn man who wouldn't listen to reason. "Look, Emilio," he said. "It's only a mountain. Leave it be. It was there before us and it will remain long after we are gone."

Emilio finished the drink Luís had proffered.

"Just a mountain, you say." Emilio spoke with finality. "We put ourselves into the soil here, our sweat and hard work. Just like our parents and grandparents before us. This is where we will all be buried. The mountain is part of us, just as we are part of the mountain. We are like the black stones of Pico."

Luís sighed. "So why climb? Pico is difficult. It's dangerous. People fall, they die."

"Because this butterfly has found a secret place where there are no others. It lives there alone, and perhaps it can only live in that one place. Anyway, I've decided I want to see them for myself before I die."

"This mountain is not for someone to go climb alone," Luís insisted. He mentioned the various people who had disappeared while attempting to climb Pico over the years, scientists and even experienced climbers who had gotten lost or fallen. "There are too many dangers," Luís said. Fog or clouds that came up without warning; *furnas* or craters that one could stumble into and fall hundreds of feet; the treacherous steep slopes.

"I've heard all that," Emilio said, waving away the so–called dangers. "People lose their way because they think they can conquer the mountain, right? But me, I go with a purpose, a search."

It was impossible. Emilio wouldn't listen. Not to his friends, not to Father Silva after Sunday Mass. He was going.

"Think of your wife and family," Father Silva said. "If God had meant for men to climb mountains—and you, an old man already. You are sick. Here is where you belong, with your family, your friends."

But nothing could shake Emilio's desire.

On the second night after his return from Terceira, Emilio kissed his sleeping children and grandchild good–bye. He walked out of the house, his traveling bag weighed down with some food, a jug of water, and a heavy rusted chain he had purchased for next to nothing from Claudio, the mechanic. He also carried the butterfly net that the naturalist had kindly given him, after Emilio had told the man that he too would climb Pico and find the butterflies that could live nowhere else.

"Can't you at least go when it's light?" Maria Alice pleaded. "Soon there will be rain, or perhaps snow. You could freeze up there."

"No. It is at night that the mountain bares its face. The clouds come with the sunrise." He kissed Maria Alice good–bye and held her briefly. "I will come back tomorrow." He started walking down the road.

"*Butterflies!*" he heard her say as he walked off. "What will I tell the children?"

"Tell them to look up at the mountaintop," he shouted. "If the weather is clear perhaps they will see me dancing with the butterflies."

The moon was full and Pico stood out, a dark tower jutting into the night, more felt than seen. Emilio was accompanied up the mountain by the sound his shoes made as they ground against the volcanic rock. On the side of the road he found a long, sturdy branch to use as a walking stick.

He climbed steadily, pausing now and again to rest or drink a bit of water. Up ahead the dark mountain loomed, always there, larger than life.

I'm coming, my friend. You don't seem so dangerous, so terrible. Just a mountain, eh?

It was true that over the years people had lost their way and disappeared, never to be seen again. But he had lived and worked his whole life here. Surely the mountain knew him as well as he knew the mountain.

He quickly left behind the houses and people, the cows, the patches of woods. Then it was only Emilio and the naked mountain. He listened to the wind rush down the slope—making a low, mournful howl as the air sang through the ravines and over the *furnas*, like blowing air across a bottle top.

"Ah, Pico is breaking wind," Maria Alice would have said. Emilio chuckled.

The path was steep and wound its way in a series of sharp switchbacks. He heard the sound of his breathing and occasionally rocks falling. The air was dry and smelled of the volcano, which slept, though no one knew when it might awaken. Now and then there had been rumbles, earthquakes.

He pushed himself to go farther, to ignore the thinning air and the steep passes, fearing that if he stopped, he might not be able to continue.

Emilio set himself landmarks to use as goalposts.

I will walk to that jutting rock up ahead before I stop. Then, after, to that crest, or that bend in the trail.

After a couple of hours he stopped and sat down to rest. He picked out the sharp stones that had lodged in the soles of his thin shoes and wiped the abrasions on his hands with a handkerchief.

You may have sharp teeth, mountain, but don't think that will stop me. I will not be turned back so easily.

Already he was tired, the climb more difficult than he had foreseen, and his body weaker, always weaker.

The lights from Faial, across the channel, blinked at him in the distance; he saw their ghosts on the dark surface of the water. He also could make out scattered lights on the island of São Jorge. Up at the top, the naturalist had said, you could see the others too: Terceira, Graciosa, almost all of the Azores with one glance. Up where the butterflies lived, hovering around the warm mountaintop; where steam escaped through cracks, steam from the very heart of the mountain.

Emilio took out some bread and a slice of meat, then ate, looking down at the world below.

It is so wide. Up here you can see there is so much nothingness out there.

The wind blew, low and mournful.

Such a sad voice you have, mountain.

After half an hour he continued walking. The paths were steep and treacherous, along cliffs and over rocks where there was poor footing and barely anything to hold on to.

Go on, make it difficult. You won't stop me. What are you hiding up there, eh?

He whistled a tune and wished he had better eyesight.

Ah, it's cold. Though thank God for the full moon. That and the fact that the skies are as clear as they have been in ages. There are not even birds up here.

His legs began to ache. The satchel felt heavier with each step, slowing him down.

This is nothing, too. Old bones, a tired body, but I have the strength to finish this. That is important. To have the will to make this climb.

Emilio kept moving. He told himself it was just around the next turn; one more ridge, and he would soon be there. Where many people half his age couldn't make it—where the scientist from the continent had found the butterfly that lived in its secret place.

He pushed himself onward, pressing down on his knees, forcing them to take another step. His breath came quickly and cut through his throat, his lungs.

Not too far. Keep going old man. You can't stop, now!

The mountain stood by, silent, imposing. On occasion, Emilio's feet would slip on the rocks, and he would hug the mountain closer.

What it must be to be as old as you are, eh, mountain? You do not die, like an old man. How many have you killed, I wonder?

The sky began to lighten. Dawn was breaking. Looking down, he saw the enormous shadow the mountain cast upon the surface of the ocean. Still, the volcano rose before him, its peak beyond reach, as if for each step he took the summit moved farther away.

How can butterflies live in such a place? There are no trees or plants. Could the man have lied, like Luís said? Why would he tell me if it wasn't true? Did he think I would never climb to find out, that it was safe to tell an old fool like me there was something here when there wasn't? Maybe I was crazy to do this.

He paused and glanced at the ocean as the sun rose. Perhaps, he thought, the clouds will come. A storm could come without warning to the mountain. He pushed on, determined to reach the top, though the pain made his movements difficult.

Emilio strained, using his arms and hands against the rocks, to get past them, to pull himself up and over. He looked down but could no longer see much below, only the sea, which appeared so calm, so smooth. He smiled happily; he was with God now.

Maybe the mountain is God's big toe.

The trail wound its way around the edge of the mountain, then cut back into sheltered ground, so unlike the rest of Pico, which was barefaced. Emilio headed for that spot, frantic to reach his goal.

Ah, it is like a nest there in the mountain, a good spot for me to find shelter.

Inside the cut, the wind was quieter and the air was warmer. He could see the peak jutting up ahead of him. The top was very near.

He waved his arms at the cone of the volcano. "Hey, look! I made it, mountain. What do you think now?"

He put the heavy satchel down and suddenly felt weightless; even his clothes, which flapped in the breeze, seemed heavier than he did now. He was glad he had brought the chain. The winds on the mountain could be fierce. The chain would weigh him down—keep his body from being blown away, like a dried leaf.

He explored the large protected area. There were no trees, but he did find some brush and small plants, and even small pools of water.

There was a sudden shift of light, and he was momentarily blinded. The sun had moved from behind Pico, filling the area with sunlight. He rubbed his eyes. Everything was a soft blur.

A column of smoke rose from the crater beyond him. On occasion the islanders had witnessed a thin plume of smoke rising from Pico's summit. Emilio even remembered a time when the smoke had formed a distinct cross. People had photographed the sight, which became a famous postcard. Now he watched the smoke rise, then spiral down toward him, as if blown by a sudden gust of wind—although he felt no wind.

Gray flakes swirled and fell around him. He reached out his hand. *Snow? Dry snow falling in sunlight?*

The flakes danced around his head. Emilio smiled. No, not snow—butterflies. A cloud of a thousand gray butterflies. The man hadn't been lying after all. He reached into the satchel and brought out the net that the naturalist had given him. The butterflies flapped their silent wings. The sun shone all around now, and he could see that some of the butterflies were violet, some yellow, while others were streaked in red, green, and blue.

Emilio peered down the mountain, toward the distant villages where his family and friends went about their lives. But everything had gone gray, nothing was clear. Still, he wondered: Did they stop and look up, gazing at the mountain, wondering about old Emilio?

"Hey, you down there. I don't need to die with you. Up here, I have wings!" He laughed and jumped up and down. Gone was the pain.

A shadow moved across the sky, and he saw that the clouds had indeed come. The butterflies flew around him, encouraging him to join them in their flight. He grabbed hold of the chain. He wrapped one end around his right leg.

Death belongs down there, he thought, not up here where strange butterflies dance around a smoking volcano, as if coming from the earth itself. He swung the net, but they flew right through it. So many, that some kept falling to the ground, in layer after layer. Just like snow.

FRANK X. GASPAR

Frank X. Gaspar is the author of five collections of poetry and two novels. Among his many awards are the Morse, Anhinga, and Brittingham Prizes for poetry, multiple inclusions in *Best American Poetry*, four Pushcart Prizes, a National Endowment for the Arts Fellowship in Literature, and a California Arts Council Fellowship in poetry. His work has appeared widely in journals in the U.S. and Portugal, including *The Nation*, *The Harvard Review*, *The Kenyon Review*, *Neo*, *Mundo Portugues*, and others. His debut novel, *Leaving Pico* was a Barnes and Noble Discovery Prize winner, a recipient of the California Book Award for First Fiction and a *New York Times* Notable Book (paperback edition). His second novel *Stealing Fatima* was a *Massachusetts Book of the Year* in Fiction. He most recently held the Helio and Amelia Pedrosa/Luso–American Foundation Endowed Chair at the University of Massachusetts, Dartmouth, and he is Editor at Large for Tagus Press. His newest collection of poems, *Late Rapturous*, was published by Autumn House in 2012.

Black Notebook, #5, Lisbon

Where sleep kept itself across the room like a long sheet
of glass, and he lay on the white bed sifting through the ash
and raking over the cinders of one burned–out dream or
another, as if he would ever find a shy feather from the angel's
wing there, no sweet or bitter powder to stop all the circling
in his head, all that grinding over and over, yielding up nothing,
and down in the street some marvelous and bejeweled girls
calling out to one another, and car doors slamming outside
the trendy club with its drift of icy music. They had gone looking
for Pessoa and found him on coffee mugs and tee shirts, They had
gone singing for Eça and Florbela and found cobblestones and
tiled walls and the bayonet rails of the crimson trolleys. How
far will any voyage take you? You can follow Roget and see how
the slap is the first glance toward murder. You can misread
the physicists and believe that hope and despair are the same
string vibrating. Love what you will quickly. You can never
stay. Deliverance never looks like itself. Weary and homeward,
then, outbound, the hard–won tickets, and the baggage groaning
with holy books in every language, the great Atlantic cloud cover,
glacial and complete, showed the curvature of the round earth and
they all wept in at least one of the rooms of the heart, for they were
all leaving *something*, each of them, unguessable and sovereign in
the deepest vault, or profound in those arcane inner whirlwinds
of marvel and fatigue. How much later then, in his little canted
rooms, home, still with the delicacies and caresses of his own
descent in the November sun. Now the nodding maple crowning
in his high windows, boughs pressing in on him, like the nose of a
lost cat against a door, all hope and resolve that the house and its
joys will open. In that moment of common fusion he saw himself
reaching through the windowpane and petting its leaves, already
cold and mortal, and the south–facing limbs easing into their final
rusts and crimsons. As if he could pass through anything, he put
out his hand but then only laid the flat of it against the glass. It was
deeply cool, surprising in the drench of westering light, and he left
his palm there for a while against a billion molecules, once opaque

and blind but now because they had joined in fire he could look through them clearly as if through one single bright jewel, and he believed in this way he could see many pieces of the scattered world.

The Sermon of Saint Anthony to the Fish
(preached in São Luis do Maranhão, 1654)

Wind off the harbor at five A.M. Sky still black in the west–facing
window, already the little streets are sounding with work—metal
banging on concrete down at the docks, an engine, a distant whistle
high and thin. Here in my attic rooms I am pacing and sitting with
Saint Anthony as he talks to the fish. He has turned away from his
congregation since they do not ever listen to him. He turns his
back on them. He summons the fish. They come. They are such
charmed fish. They listen and nod with their heads just out of
the water. They wiggle their tales. They are rapt. *The first thing
that distresses me about you fish,* he says, *is that you eat each other!*
I open the windows over my bed and then the windows over the
table and the breeze is snappy and rinses right on through, over
the planks and under the angled eaves. That's how funny Saint
Anthony is. He does not like the Octopus, but one has to mark that
off to a certain temporal prejudice—all that sneaky changing of
color and all those weird arms—certainly in service of darkness. Oh,
he must use men as parables to the fishes! How else to get them to
see their errors? But in the end he tells all those shining cod, bass,
and haddock that his words will really do them no good, no matter
that they are so attentive and sweet, so responsive and appreciative.
They have no souls, after all. The whole notion of redemption does
not apply, so their sermon can not end in grace and glory for them.
I'm still at it, after coffee, with the sun up, and the wind easily now
in the higher registers of small–craft–warning, though I cannot make
out the pennants from here. Soon the school kids come lining up
across the narrow street. Women yell at them continually, *get on
a line, get on a line.* Then they sing songs. When the children do not
understand something the women yell louder. Then they say things
again in Portuguese. It makes a music under the wuthering maples and
chestnuts and oaks. Now the light is everywhere, and the roof over my
head thumps with wind. The street is adazzle. The day opens up. I make
more coffee. You can always save something. Sometimes the riches pelt
over you like a hard rain—you duck your head and try to shelter your–
self from them because you don't see them for what they are. Even

Saint Anthony, though the fish are not capable of glory, gives them this: *Benedicite, cete et omnis quae moventur in aquis. Praise God because He has created so many of you, Who has distinguished you with so many species, Who has dressed you in such variety and beauty, Who has given you such a vast and pure element, Who, coming into this world has lived among you.* In the end, this seems just about enough for anybody.

September 10th—Black Notebook #2

I was sitting up on the graves in Provincetown, my back against the old *Gaspar* stone, and I could feel my grandfather angry and restless and hating to be dead. He wanted to laugh and walk along the wharves and streets and be greeted and hailed and loved, and drink cheap wine again. I should have brought that *other* stone with me, the black lava rock from Pico Azores that I plucked from the beach outside of what is maybe the little village that all the old ones harbored from, how I could push it into the sandy earth and cover it over and something at last would be *done*. One day I will bear it here. Another day I will fall here like blown dust. I took a bottle of green wine and opened it and poured some out and let it sink into the ground. Then I drank some, and then I poured some more on the graves, like that, back and forth, and I talked out loud to the dead, some going back so far I knew almost nothing about them but had only the gravure on the weathered granite to steer by. Sometimes to get to the new Eden you have to step on the head of the dragon. That much was written somewhere. All these gardens and forests of death. So beautiful in the light. Light everywhere and the old stones gleaming over the burying fields, white and gray, little tufts of spiky grass nestled here and there. What is the moral order of stone that it has so much to do with how love never knows where its limits are or when to stop in this world with all its perennial Gomorrahs and Jerusalems wedged flagless in the heart? Your heart and mine. Do you dream? Do you ever hear the sea? Are you broken? Are you whole and upright? The women here love God every day in their long garments, and lean over the white fences eternally and whisper to one another. The men are all hoarse and sinewy and hard at work. Somewhere in the Atlantic of mysteries it is snowing, and they are in the boat, long and narrow, heaving and shouting at the oars. The distance closes, they are making way. When I hear them, I *hear* them, but I don't know all the words. The snow aslant, the ocean fierce and peaked and black. Yet there are no impediments to their perpetual coming. By one oarlock, an empty space on the thwart. Laid along the freeboard a single clean oar. One day I will bruise my head. Another day I will bruise my heel.

Black Notebook, Psalm 15, Dead Sea Scrolls, New Bedford

The fall sun on the pitched roof of the ancient schoolhouse across the street, its chimneys and skylights, gulls crying over on the docks, bricks and moldings all alight, and I was in the breeze and under the maple tree and the ivy wall watching Thomas and Peter and John raise the dead, sometimes in multitudes, and the pages shuffling now and then in the little gusts of wind up from the harbor. Every flower may be found here. Every temple withstands the dark cloud. Cobblestones ballasting the terrible ships from London, Liverpool, Lisbon, Barbados, Joppa, Tarshish. The old iron rails of the vanished trolleys, occulted in years of asphalt, uprising now, gleaming black as starlings as they slowly shoulder sunward again, and the starlings in the trees shivering the wind away and staring eternally into the one moment. Then down among the trawlers, all muscle and steel in their high freeboard, the palisades of scoured decks, the drags rolled, the hawsers lashed tight. *The Nancy Ann, The Sea Hag, Perpetua, Little Johnny, Eight Bells, Florabella, Sculley-Joe.* The Sunday Carillon proclaiming the rapture, searching for the resolving chord the way a certain kind of man might walk among that distant angelus feeling numbly for the one scrap of grammar that could make this world click suddenly into another world. Some junction that might be untouchable by death and indelible under the false joys of the empire. What makes all the old lies so beautiful? Simon Magus, it is told and told, was seen all over Rome, flying, by hundreds of upturned faces. But when he raised the dead it was a trick, and Peter made him fall and break his leg in three places, and he died later of the wounds in the care of a false healer. You cannot make this go away no matter how many wreathes you lay at the gray tombs. When I came home the back way, crossing and wandering the narrow streets, I passed a worn-down stone building that might have been a church once, hulking, the color of fog, and I walked into a group of men on the sidewalk. They seemed to be waiting for something. Some were smoking, some were sitting on the curb and on the steps of the building. Some were speaking Island Portuguese and Cape Verdean patois. I looked into their faces. Someone asked me how I was doing. All right, I said. All right. We talked until a red-faced man opened a big door from the inside, saying nothing, but the men slowly turned and shuffled up the steps. I stayed behind and thought about everything for a moment, but by then the light had lengthened in deep angles, golden from the west, and the wind had settled into a steady blow snapping some long flags on a nearby porch, and so I didn't go in.

ABOUT THE EDITORS

Luis Gonçalves specializes in Lusophone cultures and civilizations and their transatlantic dynamic. He holds a Ph.D. in Romance Languages, with a Minor in Communication Studies and a Certification in Cultural Studies, from the University of North Carolina at Chapel Hill. He has organized several conferences and conference panels and presented papers in Portugal, Brazil, Canada and the United States, and he is also an active member of the academic community in different capacities. Luis is the editor of the blog PortugueseAmericanReview.com and also the Book Review Editor for *Gávea–Brown – a Bilingual Journal of Portuguese American Letters and Studies*. He has published book reviews and articles on several authors. His research interests include Diaspora, migrations and migrant communities, in particular from Portugal, Cape Verde and, more recently, from Brazil to the United States and Canada. In recognition of the work done in the advancement of the Portuguese language in the United States, he was awarded a prize in 2010, given by the Universidade dos Açores, Portugal, and the Portuguese World Language Institute at Lesley University, Cambridge, Massachusetts.

Carlo Matos is an Azorean–American writer who has published five books. His new book, *The Secret Correspondence of Loon and Fiasco* is now available from Mayapple Press. He has also published poems, stories, and essays in many journals like *Iowa Review, PANK, Another Chicago Magazine, Paper Darts, DIAGRAM*, and the *Gavea–Brown Book of Portuguese–American Poetry*. Carlo has received grants from the Illinois Arts Council, the Fundação Luso–Americana (FLAD), and the Sundress Academy for the Arts. He is also a recent winner of the Heartland Poetry Prize. He currently lives in Chicago, IL and teaches at the City Colleges of Chicago and the Rooster Moans Poetry Coop. A former fighter, he now trains and coaches cage fighters and kickboxers. After hours he can be found entertaining clients at the Chicago Poetry Bordello and writing poems on demand for Poems While You Wait. Follow him on twitter @CarloMatos46 or at his blog carlomatos.blogspot.com.

www.ingramcontent.com/pod-product-compliance
Lightning Source LLC
Chambersburg PA
CBHW021037030726
47496CB00006B/1573